# HOW TO DEAL WITH DIFFICULT PEOPLE

Ursula Markham is a practising hypnotherapist and business training provider. In addition to running her own successful clinic, she gives lectures and conducts workshops and seminars in Britain and abroad. She has appeared frequently on radio and television and is Principal of The Hypnothink Foundation, an organization responsible for training hypnotherapists and counsellors to professional level.

D0367488

*By the same author:*

Alternative Health – Hypnosis (Optima)
Discover Crystals (Aquarian Press)
Elements of Visualisation (Element Books)
Hypnosis Regression Therapy (Piatkus)
Managing Stress (Element Books)
Women under Pressure (Element Books)

URSULA MARKHAM

# How to Deal
# with Difficult People

## Thorsons
*An Imprint of* HarperCollins*Publishers*

Thorsons
An Imprint of HarperCollins*Publishers*
77–85 Fulham Palace Road,
Hammersmith, London W6 8JB

Published by Thorsons 1993
9 10

© Ursula Markham 1993

Ursula Markham asserts the moral right to
be identified as the author of this work

A catalogue record for this book
is available from the British Library

ISBN 0 7225 2764 0

Phototypeset by Harper Phototypesetters Limited,
Northampton, England
Printed and bound in Great Britain by
Caledonian International Book Manufacturing Ltd, Glasgow

All rights reserved. No part of this publication may be
reproduced, stored in a retrieval system, or transmitted,
in any form or by any means, electronic, mechanical,
photocopying, recording or otherwise, without the prior
permission of the publishers.

# Contents

To my family

- with all my love

# Introduction

Difficult people exist in all areas of our lives. They cause problems for anyone who comes into contact with them. This book is designed to help you understand and handle such people effectively and to get the best possible result out of any involvement with them.

As a counsellor I spend a great deal of my time helping those who consult me on how to cope with and improve the situations that come about because of other people's difficult attitudes and behaviour. As a business training provider I run seminars on dealing with difficult co-workers, superiors or subordinates. The ideas and techniques suggested in this book are based on the experience I have had in both these fields. They make a good starting-point if *you* find yourself having to cope with difficult people; you can then adapt these techniques to suit both your own personality and the particular problems you have to face – after all, no two situations are identical.

Of one thing you can be confident: understanding what makes difficult people tick and learning how best to handle them will reduce your stress and make your life a great deal easier.

# All things are difficult before they are easy

Thomas Fuller, *Gnomologia* no. 560

# CHAPTER ONE

# Understanding Yourself and Others

There is no way you can make difficult people change and suddenly become sweet and amenable. Such change can only take place when the individuals concerned desire it and work towards it. So, if you can't change *them*, the only thing to do is to change your own *reaction to them*. After all, you are the one who gets hurt and upset while they themselves simply blunder on in their own way.

All communication consists of reaction and counter-reaction. So, by changing *your* reactions – both inwardly and on the surface – you will in fact make these difficult people counter-react differently (even if only temporarily). Even if this does not help you to eliminate completely any problems that arise, it will diffuse most situations and therefore make them far easier to deal with.

Sometimes you will have to be quite skilful in the way you handle difficult people. While you can let yourself go and shout at a brother or sister, you are likely to get into trouble if you react in the same way to your boss. Even with members of your family, however, shouting is not a very good way to handle trying situations – but at least you won't lose your job!

Each of us reacts in a different way to such awkward people because each of us has a different starting point. No two individuals have the same view of themselves; one may be calm and composed, another over-confident, while a third may have very low self-esteem. It is so easy to be hurt, deflated and demoralized by the words and actions of others; indeed, this is what they rely on and what gives them their power. But if you allow them to get to you, all you are doing is letting them win – and that is not good for you nor for their next unfortunate victim. The way to overcome the difficulties that arise is to be more clever than they are and to influence their responses – and often you can do this without them even realizing what you are doing.

## How Do You React?

Perhaps it would be a good idea to look first at your own reactions to people. The instinctive retort, while often an understandable reaction is not always the best one from any point of view. Difficult people are so used to employing a particular set of tactics that you are likely to fall right into their trap and enable them to play their final trump card. As far as you are concerned, you are likely to end up feeling angry, frustrated and disappointed in yourself. Better by far to take time to think *before* you react – and better still if you have worked out your strategy in advance.

If you know that you are dealing with someone who is always difficult and who treats everyone in the same way, do try not to take personally the way he speaks to you. It is not really *you* who is being attacked; this person's attitude would be the same whoever was at the receiving end. This does not excuse the behaviour in any way – but it might help to reduce your own feelings of inadequacy.

Ask yourself what sort of reaction you have to a difficult person you know. Do you respond extremely negatively? If so, for what reason? Stop and think rationally of what your course of action should be. Simply blowing up and having a fierce verbal battle achieves nothing; all it does is bring you down to the level of the person causing all the difficulties.

You can choose how to react and respond to people. Working through this book will help you understand the choices available to you and to decide which one is best and most appropriate in a particular case. You will be able to build on your inherent strengths (and hopefully minimize your weaknesses) so that you do not allow yourself to be triggered into a response that gets you nowhere and leaves you feeling drained and disappointed in yourself.

All this does not mean that you have to become a 'yes-person' or to give in to those who are trying to influence the way you behave. It does not even mean that you are not allowed to be angry. Of course you are. Anger is a natural and often justified emotion and there is nothing wrong in feeling it; what's important is how you deal with it and express it. There is a world of difference between flying into a screaming rage and telling the other person (in a calm, controlled manner) 'I feel angry about that.' The latter is the *assertive* way and is far more effective as your listener is more likely to take notice. If you scream and shout, he will simply scream back and in the end neither of you will take any notice of what the other is saying.

To throw some light on how difficult people make you react as you do, try asking yourself the following questions:

## Do You Really Want to Be Controlled by Others?

All too often that is what is happening – and the only one to suffer is you. The difficult person will carry on, happily convinced that he has won once again.

Picture this scene: Tom is driving steadily along the main road out of town when another vehicle overtakes him on the approach to a bend and, because of oncoming traffic, is forced to cut in immediately in front of him. Tom, who has naturally had a shock, is furious. He goes scarlet with rage, bangs his steering wheel with his fist and calls the other driver every bad name he can think of. The rest of his journey is ruined because he is fuming about what happened – and what could have happened. His concentration lapses and his own driving suffers as a consequence. This makes other people sound their horns at him, which does nothing at all to improve his humour.

No one is saying that Tom was not right to be angry. He did nothing wrong; the fault was entirely the other driver's. And, had he not managed to cut in front of Tom's car when he did, the situation could have been even worse due to the stream of oncoming traffic. But who was the one to suffer for Tom's reaction? Not the other driver – who probably went on overtaking every vehicle ahead of him and was probably completely oblivious of Tom and his feelings.

No, the one to suffer was Tom. It was Tom whose blood-pressure went through the roof; Tom who was left shaking with fury; Tom who became so agitated that his own driving became far less steady and who could have, therefore, caused an accident himself. He had allowed himself and his judgement to be affected by the stupid actions of someone else – and he had not even had the satisfaction of telling that other person how he felt.

In just the same way, if you allow yourself to be goaded into a stressed and extreme reaction by the manipulative behaviour of other people, the only one you are going to harm is yourself. And not only will you fail to get the response you desire but you will be left feeling exhausted by your emotions and disappointed in your own behaviour.

## What Is Your Reaction When Confronted by Someone Who Is Furious with You?

Do you match anger with anger? Do you become defensive and make excuses – to which the other person does not listen? Or do you back off and slink away? Each of these reactions is a negative one, whether your anger is justified or not. You are also likely to be left feeling annoyed, not only with the other person but with yourself for acting in the way you have.

## Do You Talk Yourself into a State of Negativity?

You know the sort of thing: 'I'm dreading that interview – I always make a fool of myself' or 'I really hate Mondays.' If an interview is approaching, all you can do is prepare yourself as best you can and try to be as calm as possible on the day. As for Mondays – there was one last week and there's going to be one next week as well, so you might as well get used to them.

This sort of negative feeling wastes so much time. Whether the interview (or the Monday) goes well or not, you will have spoiled the intervening time by spending it in a state of dread.

## How Do You Respond to Criticism?

There are some people who just love to criticize others. It makes them feel good and gives them a sense of power. Like the bully who will only torment an obvious victim, the more response the critic gets from the object of his remarks, the more he will continue. And, also like the bully, critics tend to be moral cowards; putting others down helps them to disguise their own insecurities and have an inflated opinion of themselves. (I am not talking here of genuine, concerned criticism given in a constructive way but of those who enjoy making other people feel small).

Is your immediate response to such criticism to become defensive? Or perhaps you assume that the critic must be right (how he would love that) and take all his comments to heart without stopping to analyse their validity. As you will discover, there are ways of stopping the malicious critic and dealing assertively with the situation.

## Do You Have a Permanently Negative Outlook?

Tell yourself often enough that 'Everything has gone wrong since I moved into this house' and it will continue to do so. Convince yourself that you are having 'one of those days' and you will. Not only will your own negativity make you see only the down side of every event, it will also draw out the negativity in others.

If you find yourself behaving in this way, it is worth stopping and taking stock of the realities of your situation. What really has gone wrong since you moved into your house? Make a list and study it. Are some of the items on the list things that would have happened anyway, wherever you were living? Are they all really as bad as all that? Now make a list of all the things that have gone *right* since you came to live there – things you may not have stopped to consider from the depths of your negative hole. Great or small, I'm certain that if you are honest you will be able to find a number of things to put on the positive side. (For one thing, you are well enough to be sitting there making the list.)

Even when you look at that list of 'wrongs', can it all really be the fault of the house, the day, the weather – or whatever else you have convinced yourself is to blame? Try being more positive and making a note of good things as they happen to you – even the little ones. It really works.


## Do You Swallow Your Feelings – Both Good and Bad?

Do you find it difficult to say 'I love you' or 'I'm disappointed in what you did'? Of course you may be able to say one and not the other. Many people have been brought up to think that they have to be polite and not do or say anything to upset anyone else. That is fine – but not when it means accepting poor manners or shoddy workmanship. There is nothing wrong in expressing what you feel provided you do so in a way that is productive rather than aggressive. You will never lose your true friends – and those people who aren't true friends don't matter anyway.

Disguising your emotions only ends up hurting you. It causes a build-up of stress as you turn your feelings in on yourself rather than dealing with them. Your opinion of yourself will become ever lower as your sense of inadequacy increases. You will also cause problems for yourself in that others (particularly those difficult people) will either fail to notice you at all or will consider you a prime target.

## Perhaps You Believe in Saying What You Think Regardless of the Consequences?

Just stop for a moment and consider how you feel when other people act in such a way. Do you really want to cause others pain or distress?

Saying what comes into your head without considering the effect it will have on those around you will eventually turn others away from you. You are likely to end up believing that you are alone against the world. This is a sad enough feeling at any time but even worse if you realize that you brought it on yourself. You could find yourself trapped on a downward spiral of emotion from which it will be hard to emerge.

# Know Your Personality Type

While conducting research into the effects of stress upon the heart, cardiologists Dr Meyer Friedman and Dr Ray Rosenman divided people into Type A and Type B personalities. They found that, even if work and living conditions were identical, Type A people were three times more likely to suffer from a stroke or heart attack, as these people were more likely to react aggressively to people and situations and therefore more likely to suffer from excess stress.

Check the lists that follow and see whether you incline more towards Type A or Type B. The ideal, of course, would be to fall somewhere in between the two. It can be fine to have a 'laid-back' attitude to life – but not if you constantly miss opportunities or irritate others because of it. And a certain amount of enthusiasm and ambition is laudable – but not if it causes you to ride rough-shod over all and sundry.

These lists are meant to be a guide to whether you lean too much one way or the other. Don't be concerned if you have a few of the Type A characteristics – it probably means that you are good at getting things done. But if more than half of them apply, it might be time to see what you can do to change some of your reactions to life – before you do yourself any real harm.

## Type A Personality

- Highly competitive
- Has a strong, forceful personality
- Does everything quickly
- Anxious for promotion at work or for social advancement
- Desires public recognition for what he has achieved
- Is easily angered by people and events
- Speaks rapidly
- Feels restless when compelled to be inactive
- Likes to do several things at once
- Walks, moves and eats quickly
- Is made impatient by delay
- Is very conscious of time – thrives on having to meet deadlines
- Is always on time
- Has taut facial muscles and/or clenches fists

## Type B Personality

- Not competitive – at work or play
- Has an easy-going, relaxed manner
- Does things slowly and methodically
- Is relatively content with present work situation
- Is satisfied with social position
- Does not want public recognition
- Is slow to be aroused to anger
- Can enjoy periods of idleness
- Speaks slowly
- Prefers to do one thing at a time
- Walks, moves and eats in a leisurely way
- Is patient – not easily upset by delay
- Is not time conscious; tends to ignore deadlines
- Is frequently late
- Has relaxed facial muscles/does not clench fists

# Why Are You as You Are?

Whatever your personality and however you react to difficult people, the pattern will have been set many years ago, probably in early childhood. People and events over which you had no control will have conspired – often unwittingly – to create the self-image with which you have grown up. And if you are someone who finds it impossible to stand up to difficult people or to handle them in a satisfactory way, your self-esteem is likely to be lower than it should be. The good news is that it does not have to stay that way. It is possible at any stage in life to improve your self-image and increase your confidence.

Let's have a look at some of the most common reasons for a poor self-image and see whether you can relate to any of them.

The first people with whom you formed any kind of relationship were your mother and father (or those who stood in that position). From their attitude towards you and their opinion you will have formed a view about yourself and your 'value'. Some parents, of course, are deliberately unkind to their children, inflicting mental, physical or emotional damage. Fortunately, however, such parents make up only a small minority. But it is all too possible for the kindest and most well-meaning of adults to inflict harm, too – although they would probably be shocked if they knew they had done so. Those who are over-protective, doing everything for their child and fighting all his battles, may create an adult who has learned to be so dependent that he is quite unable to stand on his own feet. Those who care and provide for their children but find it difficult to be demonstrative (possibly due to defects in their own upbringing) may cause those children to believe that they are unworthy of love and affection – unlovable in fact.

A small child will think that his parents know everything and are perfect in every way. If one or both of those parents does not show love and affection, the child will form the inner belief that he is unworthy of such love and his self-esteem will develop (or not) accordingly. Similarly, the adult who thinks he will spur his child on by telling him that he is 'stupid' or 'could do much

17

better' will, in fact, demolish the poor child's belief in himself and his abilities until he either refuses to try or sets about everything in so half-hearted a fashion that he is bound to fail – thereby reinforcing the already negative self-image.

There may be elements in a child's upbringing that are no one's 'fault' but that still have a traumatic effect on his belief in himself. If one of these 'wonderful' parents leaves home or is away for any length of time, a child will usually believe that he is to blame and that, had he been 'better', the family could have remained complete. I have had more than one patient, now adult, who can accept logically that he or she was not responsible for one parent leaving the family home but who still finds it difficult to come to terms emotionally with the guilt experienced.

Sometimes the parting is quite unintentional. Perhaps one parent has to go away to work, goes into hospital – or even dies. It's not all that long ago that a whole generation of fathers left home because they were conscripted to fight a war. The logical explanation for the leave-taking does not seem to make a difference to the young child and, unless he is handled carefully with love and understanding, a pattern of negativity about his own worth can be formed.

An unsettled childhood can also affect the future adult. If the family move home frequently during the early years so that the child is compelled to go to new schools and find new friends at regular intervals, he may grow up to find it difficult to form relationships with others. Then, when he looks around and sees (as it seems to him) that no one else has this problem, he feels inferior and inadequate where other people are concerned.

There are some children who sail happily through life at boarding school – but there are others who find it lonely, frightening and distressing. If you were part of the latter group, the traumatic effect of being sent away for so much of the time can last well beyond schooldays.

We are all programmed in some way – sometimes positively and sometimes negatively. If a child is told often enough, 'You will never be as clever as your sister,' that statement will become the truth. Think of all the people who claim 'I could never learn to speak Spanish; I'm useless at languages.' The truth is that, provided they have no real learning problems, there is no reason at all why they could not learn another language if they wish to do so. After all, had they been born in Madrid they would have been chattering away in that tongue from the age of one or two. Every time any one of us repeats a negative statement about ourselves – whether we say it aloud or simply think it – we are reinforcing this negative programming.

But if negative programming works, surely positive programming must work too. The process is the same; only the words or thoughts change. Just as it is possible to re-record over an audio or video cassette or a computer disk, you can re-record over past programming, thereby bringing about a change in your own self-image.

Why should you bother? What does it matter if your self-image is not as good as it could be? And what has all this to do with dealing with difficult people?

If you haven't a strong belief in yourself and a reasonable amount of self-esteem, you are going to accept whatever negative words others throw at you. And if you accept these words without question and without seeing the reality of the situation, you are going to be unable to respond as you should in order to cope with the situation.

## What Can You Do?

The first thing is to accept that your self-image is not fixed. Indeed it is constantly changing in ways which may even go unnoticed. You can *choose* how you want your self-image to change.

### Success vs. Failure

Try not to keep looking back at what you consider to be your failures. We've all had them. Professional footballers sometimes miss 'easy' goals; champion ice-skaters sometimes fall over – and

I bet even Einstein got his sums wrong once or twice! But none of these continued to punish himself for years afterwards or entertained the belief that he was 'no good' in a chosen field. It is only worth reminding yourself of your failures if you are to learn from them. If they show you something you did wrong and you make a decision not to do it again, that is all you need. Once that positive outcome has been reached, all you can do is let the failures go and leave them where they belong – in the past.

Create your own successes. Start in a very small way. Choose something you find it difficult to do, whether it's walking into a room full of people or jumping into a swimming pool. Now do it – but only in your imagination. Creative visualization is another way of saying that you should practise something in your imagination, always seeing it through to a successful ending, until your subconscious mind becomes so used to the image that it will cease to send out panic signals when you come to do the deed in reality.

In order to visualize effectively, you should find a quiet time of day or evening – just before going to sleep is ideal. Sit or lie quietly and allow your mind and body to relax. Now see the feared situation in your mind, as you would *like* it to be in reality. Don't just picture yourself walking into that room full of people; see yourself doing it in a calm and self-assured way. Imagine going up to someone – perhaps someone who looks ill at ease – and doing what you can to make him feel more comfortable. See yourself chatting in a relaxed manner with those whom you meet. If you repeat this process daily over a period of time (at least three weeks if possible), you will find when you come to put the action into effect that you will have successfully reprogrammed your mind for success.

## Making a 'Like-List'

Make a list of those things about yourself that you like. The person who claims that he cannot find anything to put on a list is not thinking deeply enough – or is not telling the truth. Because people with a poor self-image are usually by definition highly sensitive, it follows that they tend to be kind, compassionate and unwilling to hurt others. So there's the first thing to put on your list; now go on from there.

Once you have completed your list, look at the characteristics you have written there. If they applied to some stranger you had never met, you would not think he could be such a bad person, would you? So why are you so hard on yourself?

Instead of looking back only at negative events in your life, try remembering your successes. Everyone has had some, however small. Perhaps you won a badge in the Guides or Scouts, perhaps you bake a good cake – or perhaps you are kind to little children and animals. All of these are successes. Think of as many as you can. Don't just list them to yourself but remember how it felt to achieve them or to be praised for them. Relive those moments. If you are going to look back at the past, you might as well do it in the most positive way you can.

For some people, simply knowing the reason for their low view of themselves can be enough to help overcome it. Many of us do not take the time to think about the cause of our negativity; we just accept it as part of our nature. But, once you can see that the fault was not yours but lay in your upbringing or your early programming, you may not need to cling on to that false impression of yourself any longer.

Once you have learned to reduce self-criticism and improve your self-image, you will be less likely to suffer from the otherwise damaging words and actions of difficult people. Also, because you have learned to understand yourself better, you may also be able to understand them. You may begin to see that something has made them the way they are. Once you can begin to feel sorry for someone, however dreadful he may be, he can no longer inflict harm on you.

As your confidence grows you will also be able to put into action the techniques you are going to learn in the rest of this book to help you deal with difficult people. You will know that you are likely to succeed in coping with them and that, even on the odd occasion when you do not succeed, you will have done your best and so will have no need to reproach yourself in any way at all.

# CHAPTER TWO

# Styles of Behaviour

The majority of people with whom you come into contact, whether in your business or personal life, will exhibit one of three general styles of behaviour: they will be (mainly) either aggressive, submissive or assertive. If you are to be able to deal with people you need to be able to recognize these styles of behaviour and be armed with methods of minimizing their negative effect. An important part of doing this is making sure that you yourself are in the 'assertive' category.

Let's have a look at the three basic types and see how to recognize them instantly:

## The Aggressive Person

The aggressive person is the verbal bully, concerned only with satisfying his own needs, and frequently hurting other people in the process. (By the way, when I refer to 'he' 'his' or 'him' anywhere in this book please take it to mean either gender. No sexism is intended.)

The aggressive person enjoys the feeling of power that he thinks he has and the ability to make people rush about and do his bidding – but his enjoyment is often short-lived. He may never admit it but deep inside he knows that he is taking advantage of others who are either weaker than himself or in a position where they are unable to do anything about it – for example, when a manager is aggressive towards a very junior employee who is not able to retaliate without risking his job.

Convinced that he is the only one who could possibly be right in any situation and that the only needs that matter are his own, the aggressive person reminds others repeatedly of just how clever, strong or important he is. Just as physical bullying often hides a cowardly nature, this sort of boasting often masks feelings of inferiority or self-doubt. In addition to persuading others of his superiority, the aggressive person is also trying desperately to convince himself.

You will often find that the aggressive person is also a lonely person. His behaviour tends to drive others away in both his business and personal life. Because he has constantly to reassure himself and everyone around that he is the best, the most interesting and the most intelligent, he is excessively critical of everyone else. It is a great ego-booster for him to think that everything that goes wrong is someone else's fault, but it does not make him very popular. Although he may feel a desperate inner need to have friends, he is unlikely to admit this; you have to treat friends as equals and he cannot allow himself to admit that anyone is worthy of such consideration.

Someone who is aggressive often has a great deal of energy and vitality. If only he could learn to harness that energy and use it positively, all would be well. Sadly, he tends to use it in a destructive way rather than a constructive one. Some people mistake aggression for strength and feel that if they display any other type of behaviour they will be taken for weaklings or will seem as if they do not know their own minds.

When aggression is taken to extremes it becomes violence (physical aggression). However, we will concern ourselves only with the verbal aggressor, with whom most of us are more likely to come into contact.

Not only does the aggressive person not really like himself, he also has a negative effect on all the people around him. These others may feel angry or frustrated because, while only too aware of the unfairness of his attitude, they are either powerless to do anything about it or resent having to waste their time and energy trying to defend themselves against his unjust accusations. This waste of energy, coupled with feelings of helplessness, is quite exhausting and often causes the aggressor's 'victims' a great deal of stress and tension.

Even if those who come into the line of fire know perfectly well that the aggressor's accusations and comments are unjust and uncalled for, they will not be able to help feeling hurt and even humiliated by them. No one likes to be made to appear foolish or to be corrected in front of others – and of course this is just what the aggressive person does. It adds to his sense of power if as many people as possible can hear him exerting his authority and putting down some other 'inferior' being.

Because anticipation of an event is often more stressful than the event itself, those who have to come into frequent contact with an aggressive person may feel that they are living on the edge of a volcano, always waiting for the next eruption. At the least this can cause them to feel anxious or inhibited; at worst it can lead to excess stress which in turn can bring about physical or mental illness. But of course the aggressor rather likes the fact that all around him are waiting for the other shoe to drop. It adds to his sense of power and authority.

Taking all this into account, it is hardly surprising that everyone tends to leave the aggressive person alone if they possibly can. This increases his feelings of isolation and of being 'different' or 'special', so he is likely to act in an even more aggressive fashion, thus perpetuating the cycle.

Anyone who comes into frequent contact with an aggressor will find no difficulty in identifying him at a glance, but here are some 'give-aways' in both verbal and body language which will point him out immediately even to a relative stranger.

## Verbal Language: The Aggressive Person Will Say Things Like:

- You'd better . . .
- You're hopeless . . .

- You must . . .
- Do what I tell you . . .
- I want you to . . .
- Get on with it!

**Body Language**

- Stands still
- Has a stiff, rigid posture
- Keeps arms folded
- Shouts
- Points finger
- Stabs with finger
- Bangs desk or table

# The Submissive Person

In complete contrast, the submissive person is one who tends constantly to sacrifice his own needs in favour of other people's. He is therefore easily put upon by others – even those who are not by nature aggressive. It is just that the submissive person seems to encourage this attitude in those with whom he comes in contact.

In former generations it was believed that women were 'supposed to' behave in a submissive way; it is only comparatively recently that it has become acceptable for a woman to be assertive or competitive. Progress in this direction has been impeded, however, by men in certain organizations who are old enough or bound enough by tradition to cling to the old ideas of 'a woman's place'. In such companies it is extremely difficult for a woman, however talented, efficient and conscientious to reach the top. Presumably, however, as the members of this old hierarchy retire women will have more of an opportunity to share professional responsibilities with men.

The submissive person suffers greatly from feelings of insecurity and inferiority. His self-esteem is non-existent and he has no confidence at all in himself or in his abilities. Every time he comes into contact with an aggressor his feelings of inferiority are reinforced. He tends to accept criticism without stopping to question whether it is justified or not.

Because he realizes that he allows other people to take advantage of him – and does so repeatedly – the submissive person often experiences considerable anger. However this anger is not turned outwards towards the person or people taking advantage but inwards on himself for allowing it to happen. Yet he does little or nothing about it, believing that 'there is no point' in trying when he is 'never' going to be taken seriously or get his own way. This in turn causes great inner frustration; after all, no one really likes to feel helpless – still less if he believes he 'deserves' it.

The submissive person is normally quite good at hiding his true feelings. He carries on with life pretending that everything is fine while feeling constantly anxious, fearful that it is only a matter of time until he is 'caught out' and 'exposed' for the inadequate that he is. As you can imagine, this makes him a gift for the aggressor, who is only looking for someone to accept the blame for anything that goes wrong. What a bonus to come upon a willing victim, someone who truly believes that everything *is* his fault!

A submissive person often withdraws from others, feeling that he does not deserve to mix with these superior beings – and that they would not want to know him anyway. He believes that no one would want to listen to him because anything he might want to say would be trivial, unimportant or wrong.

Try and compliment a submissive person and you find that he is quite unable to accept it. He turns any positive statement into a negative one. For example, if you say: 'I do like that outfit; it really suits you', instead of a simple 'Thank you' the submissive person is more likely to answer 'What, this old thing? I've had it for ages,' thus making you feel foolish (i.e. negative) too.

Because of the constant stress and anxiety that surrounds him, not to mention the fear of being 'found out', the submissive person has little energy or enthusiasm for life. He has no time to spend on himself because he spends his entire time trying to do what he thinks other people want him to do.

You would suppose that everyone other than the aggressor would feel sympathy for the submissive person and want to help him have a better opinion of himself and to boost his confidence. Indeed, most people start off this way. But sympathy only goes so far – and then irritation sets in. People begin to wish he would stand up for himself for once, do what he wants to do and take some decisions for himself. When this doesn't happen others can lean towards aggressive behaviour because they lose all respect for the submissive person and treat him accordingly.

Constant contact with someone who is submissive can be quite exhausting. It takes a lot of energy to deal with someone who is always negative in word and deed. It is quite a draining experience, leaving you tired and struggling to maintain your own positivity. The outcome of all this is that most people tend to avoid the submissive person altogether unless they absolutely can't avoid him – thus adding to his feelings of isolation and inferiority.

The submissive person can also be recognized by his typical verbal and body language:

## Verbal Language

- Oh dear . . .
- I'm terribly sorry to bother you but . . .
- I wonder if you could possibly . . .
- I'm sorry; I'm really sorry . . .
- But . . .but . . .

## Body Language

- Never looks at you
- Keeps his fists clenched or wrings his hands
- Stoops
- Whines or speaks very quietly
- Steps backward when spoken to

## The Assertive Person

An assertive person is someone who is concerned for himself and his own rights as well as those of other people. He wants to meet others on an equal footing rather than score points over them.

The assertive person is usually the only one of the three types who ends up achieving the goals he has set himself. The aggressor may believe that he wins in the short term but, because he creates such bad feeling around him, there is no loyalty on which he can depend. The submissive person often does not set himself any goals in the first place, believing that he would never be able to reach them.

Respect for other people and the realization that they too have needs and rights distinguishes the assertive person from these others. His aim is for everyone to win and for this reason he is willing to negotiate and compromise in a positive way. When he makes a promise he always keeps it and so those around him develop trust in him. Because he is in touch with his own feelings, he is able to explain how he feels to others – even when his feelings are negative because of something they have done or said – and can do so in such a way that these others will feel no resentment.

Inwardly the assertive person feels at peace with himself and therefore with those around him. Each new challenge is faced in a positive rather than a negative way and, because of his inner confidence and the fact that he is aware of his own limitations, he is prepared to take a certain number of risks when it comes to new ventures and ideas. Sometimes things may not work out as he had hoped, but someone who is assertive realizes that it is permissible to be wrong occasionally and that it is possible to learn from one's mistakes. Assertiveness means that he does not have to steal anyone else's ideas or stab others in the back. When things go well he is able to acknowledge his success and be proud of – as opposed to conceited about – what he has achieved.

Outwardly the assertive person is a joy to be associated with. His enthusiasm can be catching and will often inspire others to become more positive in their outlook. Because he is not manipulative and does not go behind other people's backs, those around him learn to believe in and co-operate with him. His sense of inner serenity reduces the amount of stress he feels and he is therefore more able to direct his energy into achieving whatever goals he has set himself. And, because he rarely suffers from extreme mood swings, his behaviour towards others is consistent and the lines of communication are kept open.

Obviously, from the description above, an assertive person feels good about himself most of the time. Because of this he makes other people feel good, too. They develop a sense of security and trust because regular communication and feedback lets them know what is expected of them and where they stand. Tactical 'game-playing' or attempts to score over one another are reduced to a minimum and therefore everyone concerned is able to turn their energies towards achieving a communal goal rather than indulging in petty power struggles.

Respect is an integral part of the assertive person's attitude – respect for himself and for other people. And this respect is usually reflected around him, encouraging his colleagues to co-operate as fully as possible. Any success, great or small, is commented upon and complimented and this, too, encourages everyone to try even harder to perform well, whatever the task.

Verbal and body language by which you can recognize the assertive person include the following:

## Verbal Language

- I feel . . .
- I would like . . .
- What is your opinion?
- What do you think is the best way to tackle . . .?
- I think . . .
- Let's . . .

## Body Language

- Has an upright but relaxed stance
- His gaze is steady and he maintains eye contact
- Has a sense of composure

29

# Becoming More Assertive

It is obvious, from the descriptions of the three styles of behaviour, that you will be happier and achieve more if you can become assertive. Now, this is not going to happen overnight but the desire to change and a little effort can achieve a great deal.

Begin by tackling small problems rather than major ones. Then you will be able to register a number of successes fairly quickly instead of feeling that you are putting in a great deal of effort and achieving little. Do remember, however, to stop and give yourself credit for whatever successes you achieve, however minor. One of the attributes of the assertive person is that he is able to feel pleased with his progress.

Think of a situation where you feel that you have not acted assertively. This can be connected either with your working or home life, as developing assertiveness applies across the board. Ask yourself these questions

- What is the situation?
- Is the other person concerned aggressive, submissive or assertive?
- What has been my reaction to date?
- What would an assertive reaction be?

Even if you are not yet certain that you would be able to put this assertive behaviour plan into action (although, once you have read further, you should know just what to do), at least you will have worked out the situation, understood where any manipulation is coming from and seen the effect of reaction and counter-reaction between the people concerned.

Whatever type of person you encounter, as an assertive person you should be able to do all of the following:

1. Express your positive feelings: 'I do like your new hairstyle;' 'I love you.'
2. Express your negative feelings: 'I don't like it when you speak like that;' 'I'm frightened.'

3. Say no: 'No, I can't work through my lunch break;' 'No, I don't like Mexican food.'
4. Give an honest opinion: 'I think we should leave now;' 'I don't agree.'
5. Say that you are angry, provided that anger is justified: 'The way you do that irritates me;' 'I feel angry when you are rude to others.' (Note that saying that you are angry does not have to involve raising your voice, becoming abusive or thumping the furniture. Acknowledging the emotion and expressing it is quite sufficient for others to know where they stand).

As an assertive person you have certain rights:

- You are entitled to ask for what you want – but you also have to remember that the other person is entitled to say no.
- You are entitled to make decisions and choices for yourself.
  Because you are a human being and therefore fallible, sometimes these decisions and choices will turn out to be the wrong ones – but, as an assertive person you will be prepared to face the consequences whether they are good or bad.
- You are entitled to your own opinions and feelings, to acknowledge them to yourself and to express them to other people.
- You are entitled to make mistakes, bearing in mind that others must be allowed to make mistakes, too.
- You are entitled not to know everything.
  This does not mean that you are ignorant, foolish or a failure.
- You are entitled to decide whether you want to become involved in someone else's problems.
  As an assertive person, however close you may be to another person and however much he may try to persuade you to intervene, only you can decide whether to do so or not.
- You are entitled to change your mind.
  If your change of mind involves other people, you will do them the courtesy of informing them rather than leaving them to find out at some later date.
- You are entitled to privacy.

Everyone needs a certain amount of time and space alone, whatever his circumstances. Unfortunately it is often taken as a sign that you are unhappy with those around you. As an assertive person you will offer reassurance and explain that no such inference is intended. Of course, you will also remember that those around you are entitled to some privacy, too, and will not take offence if they express a desire to be alone at times.

• You are entitled to achieve.

If you have ideas, a positive attitude and energy, by all means combine them and achieve all you can. Provided you have not taken unfair advantage of others you should feel proud of what you have done.

• You are entitled to alter yourself in any way you choose – granting the same right to other people.

Think back over your recent past and see if you can remember a way in which you have abused your own rights. Perhaps you can say 'I never have a moment to myself' or 'I get drawn into other people's quarrels.' Be aware of your reactions to others, remember your rights and decide how you will do things differently in the future.

Becoming assertive is more than just a way of dealing with difficult people or of coping with awkward situations. It is a means of making personal progress. Whether you think that this life is all that counts or whether you believe that what we do is part of a longer and deeper evolution, personal development is essential if you are to achieve in any real sense. It is up to you to decide what you want – from a particular situation or from life in general – and then set goals and work towards them. Don't worry if success seems a little elusive at times; even slow progress is positive progress.

A non-assertive person lets life happen to him. He sits back and waits to see what occurs. An assertive person decides what he wants and sets out on the path to it. He will take some chances and make some mistakes. He will learn from his errors, picking himself up and trying again. While it may be true that if you never join in a game (i.e. take chances) you never lose – you never win, either.

## Giving and Receiving Compliments

A genuine compliment, gladly given, can give the recipient so much pleasure that it is a real pity most people find it such a difficult thing to do. Get into the habit of giving compliments – don't save them for special occasions. Whether you are informing a business colleague that you think he has performed a task particularly well or telling your daughter you love the painting she has brought home from school, you will be bringing happiness and a sense of achievement into the other person's life. The positive energy derived from a sense of achievement can spur a person on to even greater things in the future.

Thinking back to the first chapter and the way so many people have been programmed to think of themselves of failures, by helping others to consider themselves achievers you may be breaking a negative mould which has been impeding their personal progress for years. And all for the sake of a sincere compliment.

It is important, of course, that the compliments you give should be sincere. The recipient will soon see through false praise and will either doubt your honesty (and therefore lose trust in you) or think that you have some ulterior motive.

If you are going to give compliments to other people, you also have to learn how to accept them yourself. Many people tend to think of themselves as 'unworthy' or to put themselves down. How many times have you heard someone respond to a compliment with some self-deprecating comment?

'Your hair looks particularly nice today.'

'Oh, no, it looks awful really.'

All that is needed is a simple 'thank you' and a smile; then both 'complimentor' and 'complimentee' will feel satisfied.

## Making Changes

These can be changes in your appearance, behaviour, routine, goals – or in your ideas. Circumstances, other people's opinions and sometimes the media have all contributed to our preconceived ideas about those around us. Every young man clad in black leather and big boots is not a potential thug any more than every little old lady with silver hair is sweet-natured, but years of pigeon-holing may lead us to group people together based on their outward appearance.

If you are to be assertive, you need to make a commitment to change some part of yourself or your life. You might decide to change your style of clothes, to learn about a subject at evening classes or to alter your behaviour in particular situations. Start now by choosing some aspect of your life which you intend to change. Reinforce your commitment by writing down the details of your projected change:

1. What change do I intend to make?
2. What are the problems I may encounter?
3. What will be the positive benefits?
4. When am I going to begin?

## Communication

An assertive person is a good communicator. Because he recognizes the importance of the other person's opinion, he is a good listener. This involves understanding not only what is said but also all non-verbal communication (body language). He is able to begin conversations and to sustain them, speaking calmly and saying what he truly feels.

Because communication is so vital, it is important to realize that 'small talk' has its place, too. We do not have to spend our entire lives discussing matters of earth-shaking significance. More trivial chat about the weather, holidays or what the children are doing is a means of forging a link between ourselves and others. People who are unable to communicate on such a level tend only to be able to 'talk at' rather than 'talk to' others. And, since no one really wants to be lectured continuously, resentment may soon grow on the part of the listener.

## Negotiation

The ability to negotiate is an essential part of the assertive person's repertoire. If this were a perfect world and everyone in it an assertive person, negotiating and compromise would be far more common.

In order to negotiate in any situation it is necessary to understand the other person. After all, he has a right to his opinion just as much as you have a right to yours. If there is a clear indication of his feelings, show him that you are aware of it. You might say something like, 'I can see that this is worrying you' or 'I understand your point of view'. If you are at all unsure of what his position is or how he feels, don't be afraid to ask for an explanation.

Whatever happens, and even if the other person loses his temper or becomes overemotional, you must remain calm. If you feel yourself growing tense, concentrate on relaxing your muscles – particularly those around your shoulders and jaw where tension is quick to build up. Breathe deeply and steadily; this will help you to remain in control.

If you are going to negotiate you need to do so from a position of strength, so be sure that you are armed with whatever facts are necessary to back your point of view. And keep to the topic under discussion without allowing superfluous opinions or accusations to enter into the conversation. If the other person wanders off the point, gently but firmly bring him back to it.

Eventually you may reach the stage where you feel it is appropriate to propose a compromise. This is not the same thing as capitulating or acting in a submissive way. There is little point in being stubborn just for the sake of it and you will probably find it easier than you think to reach a solution that satisfies both parties without either of you feeling that you have been forced to give in against your will.

## Handling Put-downs

Unfortunately there are people who delight in making others feel small. While they should not be allowed to get away with it, an aggressive reaction will simply instigate an argument which may become heated. A submissive reaction will achieve nothing at all except possibly to cause the perpetrator to feel that he has scored a victory. Either of these responses will have the added negative effect of causing you to be annoyed with yourself afterwards.

If you come into contact with someone who enjoys delivering a good put-down, try to see the hidden inference behind his words. If he says to you, 'Haven't you done that yet?' what he is really saying is 'You're incompetent.' Unless you know that you really are at fault and have failed to do something you promised to do, a possible assertive response would be 'Not yet. When did you want it done?'

If you are aware of put-downs and recognize them for what they are – a form of bullying where the aggressor is seeking to inflate his own ego by making you feel inferior – you are less likely to fall into this trap. If you have succumbed in the past, think about it now and decide how you would react should the situation present itself again.

## Dealing with Criticism

No one really likes to be criticized. An assertive person, however, will realize that criticism falls into two categories:

- *Unfair*: If criticism is unfair, it is unimportant and you should not pay any attention to it.
- *Fair and constructive*: If the criticism is justified, although you still may not like to hear it, in the long term it can prove to be useful and positive.

Reacting aggressively to criticism causes problems of its own. If you snap back at the critic you will probably start an argument. If you are not assertive, you will not win the argument and you will end up feeling bad about it.

If you react submissively to criticism and always agree with the critic, whether or not he is being fair and just, you are simply pushing yourself lower and lower in his estimation – and in your own. Eventually you will reach the stage where you never do anything at all in case it attracts criticism from others.

There are three main techniques for dealing with criticism:

1. *If the criticism is fair* – agree with whatever is justified (although not with that which is simply judgemental) and say what you intend to do about it:

   'It was your turn to do the washing-up this morning and it's still there in the sink [criticism]; you're absolutely hopeless [judgement]'.

   'Yes, it was my turn. I'll do it right now.'

   This is not a submissive response because the criticism is a fair one. You did promise to do the washing up and you failed to do so. Your reply will serve to show the critic that you acknowledge the fault and intend to put things right. This will take the wind out of his sails and a possible argument will be avoided.

2. *If the criticism has an underlying truth but is exaggerated* – accept that which is justified but do not react in any way to the exaggeration:

   'You were supposed to have that report on my desk by 9 this morning and you still haven't finished it. You just don't care. Everyone else always ends up doing your work.' (The only true part of this criticism is likely to be the first sentence.)

   'Yes, I am late submitting the report and I'm sorry about that. I'll work through my coffee break and get it to you at the first possible moment.'

   By staying calm and responding only to the true part of the criticism, you remain in control of the situation. The critic will be appeased by your offer to go out of your way to put the matter right and, because you have not risen to the bait and responded aggressively to the unjust part of the criticism, an argument is less likely to ensue.

3. *Responding with a question* – this is a particularly useful response when someone is making a criticism of you personally as opposed to your work.

'You wouldn't understand.'

'Why do you think I wouldn't understand?'

The critic's reply to your question will help you to decide whether he is genuinely concerned about you – in which case he will go on to explain his comment – or is simply being unpleasant – in which case he is likely to begin to bluster, having nothing specific with which to back up his statement. Then you will know that he is not really worth bothering about and his remarks will cease to distress you.

## Preparation

Suppose you have to find an assertive way of persuading someone to do something. Many people find this difficult, particularly if there is an implied or actual criticism of the other person for poor performance to date. There are four points you need to cover and, bearing these in mind, it is often helpful to prepare a script in advance to ensure that each step is taken in turn. Naturally you do not need to read the script out when you come to talk to this person, but it will help you to fix in your mind what you intend to say. The four steps are:

1. Explain the current situation as you perceive it. Be brief and keep to the point without allowing extraneous judgement to creep in.
2. Show that you understand the other person's feelings and then express your own. You might say 'I feel upset about this' or 'I realize that you are in a difficult position.'
3. Say what you want, making as few demands as possible and keeping them realistic. There is no sense in making demands which it is physically impossible for the other person to deliver. In such cases (unless it is completely inappropriate) you might have to be prepared to negotiate or to compromise.
4. Explain what the outcome is likely to be, stating the rewards if she complies or the punishment if not. (Perhaps, 'I shall take my custom elsewhere.')

If you are able to analyse your own behaviour and then use the guidelines in this chapter to help yourself work towards becoming a more assertive person, you will have taken a very big step towards dealing successfully with any difficult people in your life.

# CHAPTER THREE

# Types of Problem People

Difficult people don't just have an effect on you for the length of time you are with them – they can spoil your whole day, week or month. An encounter with an expert difficult person can leave you feeling angry (with yourself as well as with him), hurt or frustrated. And you can be sure that he knows this all too well. Such people rely on having this effect on others; they do it because they know it works and helps them to manipulate other people, thus leaving them to go ahead with things in their own sweet way.

You have to realize one fact from the outset: you cannot change a difficult person just because you want to. With a few exceptions, difficult people are quite happy to be as they are. So, if you cannot change them, you need to learn a technique for dealing with them so that (i) you are not manipulated by them and (ii) you do not allow them to have a devastating effect on your own temper and behaviour.

The types I am going to discuss here are those who are perpetually presenting problems. Of course you can be difficult and so can I – but hopefully this is only on occasion. To deal with really difficult people you need first to understand them and then to work out a method of coping with them and their behaviour while maintaining your own temper and sanity. This applies whether you encounter them in your business or your personal life.

For the purposes of this chapter, I have divided difficult people into 13 basic types – although of course there will be others who fall somewhere between two personalities, exhibiting different behaviour according to the situation in which they find themselves.

# Janet

There are some people who are so wrapped up in what they are doing that they never even pause to consider anyone else's feelings or opinions. They are not necessarily deliberately negative – but they can irritate others enormously. A typical example is someone who always has the volume on the television turned up far too high and who is too thoughtless or unaware of other people to realize that this level of noise is causing them distress. If you ask this person to turn the volume down, she will probably do so immediately – but the next time she watches television she will forget and the volume will be just as high.

Janet is just such a person. She loves to chat and gossip and is one of those people who speak rapidly and without great variation in tone of voice. She also continues to talk even when the person she is talking to does everything possible to bring the conversation to an end. You might be trying to write a letter, read a book or even put on your jacket to leave – but Janet still goes on talking. Not only is this extremely irritating, it is pointless as people become so impatient that they mentally 'switch off', so whatever it is that she wants to say, no one actually takes it in.

At the office Janet is even more annoying. She will come up to her colleagues and, without pausing to discover whether or not they are busy, will hurl herself into her latest monologue until, as one of her co-workers puts it, 'you are ready to scream or to throttle her'.

Because individuals like this are not unkind or malicious but simply so concerned with what they want at any precise moment that they are oblivious to the feelings of those around them, others are hesitant to be rude or unpleasant to them. Everyone at the office would discuss Janet and wonder what could be done about her but no one did anything, until eventually Tony decided to try.

The first thing Tony did was to ask Janet to meet him for coffee, telling her he had something important to discuss with her. This served two purposes: (i) he aroused her curiosity and (ii) he made sure that when they did meet, *she* would be waiting for *him* to speak. When coffee had been served, he began by stating his ambivalence about the situation: 'I haven't really been looking forward to this discussion, Janet, though I do feel it will be beneficial. But I'm a little worried about how you are going to react.' This opening achieved two things. In the first place, it relieved some of the stress of the situation for Tony and, in the second, it made Janet determined to react kindly to whatever he said.

Tony then went on to explain how difficult people found it to work while Janet chattered on and that, although they liked her as a person, it caused them to become irritated with her. He also enabled her to save face by telling her that he was positive she simply intended to be friendly and did not realize what she was doing.

Janet was amazed. 'Do you really mean that?' she said. 'I never realized I came across in that way'.

Because, however much a person desires to change no one can break old habits overnight, Tony then offered to help her. He suggested that, if ever she unthinkingly slipped back into the old ways, he would give her a sign in order to jog her memory. Janet accepted his offer gratefully and, despite occasional lapses, did her best to modify her chattering.

### Dealing with a Janet

- Tell her you have something to say to her and make an appointment to do so.
- Make her feel kind towards you by saying you are worried about her possible reaction.
- Tell her clearly what it is that she does that irks others, but reassure her that you don't think she realizes what her behaviour is like or the problems it causes.
- Offer to help until she has broken the habit.

# Arnold

Arnold is one of those people who, whatever the situation, manages to make you feel negative and miserable.

Conversations may begin innocently enough but always end with Arnold putting you down. Sometimes there will be a specific criticism ('You never did know how to bake a cake'); on other occasions the put-down will be more general ('You're useless'). Whichever it is, the result is likely to be that you feel hurt or even actively hostile – and this can have a devastating effect on your work or relationships.

Perhaps the first thing to realize is that Arnold is someone who is basically insecure himself. He tries to cover up his own poor self-image and boost his flagging ego by criticizing others. If your response is to be submissive and to apologize or agree with his (unfair) accusations, you will simply be adding to his false sense of power. You are not going to change him – he would never admit that such a thing could be necessary. What you can do is react to him in an assertive way. If he complains that you are 'useless', ask him 'Why do you say that?' If, as is likely, he then falters or says things you know are untrue, this will help you find the strength to ignore him and will negate his negative effect upon you. Provided you remain calm, an Arnold almost always blusters when put on the spot.

Tempting as it may be, the worst thing you can do to an Arnold is retaliate in kind. An aggressive 'What do you mean – I'm useless?' or 'Well, you're useless too' will do nothing but provoke a tirade of (probably untrue) accusations and, unless you are a difficult person yourself, you will be verbally beaten into submission.

### Dealing with an Arnold

- Don't react submissively; don't apologize or agree.
- Don't snap back at him.
- Ask an assertive question.
- If he blusters, he can be ignored – his criticisms do not matter.

# Helen

Helen is like a bulldozer – noisy, forceful and ready to mow down anything in her way. A typical example of one of the most aggressive personality types, Helen is likely to shout, point her finger, wave her fist or thump the table. She is extremely disruptive in a work situation and terrible in relationships, as her need to rule and conquer overcomes any consideration for the feelings of others.

Helen's one aim is to get her own way – and she usually does. Everyone else tends to give her a wide berth or to lose his temper – and since she does that so much better than anyone else, no one stands a chance of winning. She always seems to be in command of the situation and indeed can be highly successful in the short term. In the long term, however, she is more destructive than constructive.

The unfortunate thing is that Helen is usually a clear and logical thinker who is keen and able to solve problems. Her weakness is that she tends to make snap decisions and then, right or wrong, insists on sticking to them, refusing to hear a word against her chosen path of action.

It is essential to stand up to people like Helen if you are to gain their respect – but this must be done in a calm and controlled way. Use phrases such as 'in my opinion' or 'in my judgement', indicating that you have ideas too but are not insisting that theirs are not just as valid. You can even tell them that you disagree with them, but follow this up with 'but tell me more about your ideas'.

Helen has a quick mind and will frequently interrupt you, having made up her mind what your next words will be. If this happens, stand your ground and say quietly but firmly 'You interrupted me' before going on with what you were saying. Make sure that you don't sound either angry or submissive; assertiveness is necessary to gain her respect. You will probably find that, once you have stood up to her, she actually thinks of you differently and will trust you enough to talk about whatever problems there may be.

Body language is vital when dealing with this type of person. Maintaining eye contact on an equal level is important. So, if you are seated, try and persuade her to sit. If she will not, you must rise from your seat in order to maintain that eye contact.

### Dealing with a Helen

- Stand up to her but don't get into a fight – you won't win.
- Tell her you disagree but ask her to explain her views further.
- If she interrupts you, stop her and tell her so.
- Don't sound angry or weak.
- Maintain eye contact on the same level.

# Stuart

Stuart is also aggressive – but surreptitiously so. His method of attack is to go behind other people's backs and sow seeds of discontent – always making sure that this gets back to them. Or he will say something offensive in a pseudo-humorous way so that, if offence is taken, his victim will appear to be a bad sport who cannot take a joke. Difficult as people like Helen might be, at least they are out in the open; the Stuarts of this world always fire their darts from under cover. It does not really matter whether the things they say are true or not; whichever the case, they will hurt you, upset you or cause you to look foolish. If someone like Stuart makes a joke at your expense in front of other people and those people laugh, however awkwardly, your self-esteem is bound to suffer.

To deal with a person like Stuart it is essential to get him alone. Stuarts just love an audience and are masters at playing to the crowd. Once you have such a tormentor alone, confront him and say that when he made the joke it sounded as if he really meant it. Now ask him if he did. This is very important. His most likely response will be to tell you that you are over-sensitive or that you should learn how to take a joke. Look him straight in the eye once more and ask him whether he intended to be hurtful. He will respect your assertiveness and will probably try to justify himself in order to save face.

If someone like Stuart tries to get at you behind your back, you may hear about it from a third party. In this case it is essential to persuade the third party to tell you precisely what was said. You may have to reassure her that you are not trying to get her into trouble but that you would really like to set the matter straight. Even if, after all your persuasion, the third party does not tell you what was said, at least you can be sure that *she* will never be the one to spread tales about you in the future.

If your third party does repeat what was originally said, you must go back to source and tell him what you have heard. Ask him if it is accurate. If he says 'no', say that you will set the other person straight. If he says 'yes' then, as before, ask him whether he intended to be hurtful and, whether he did or not, to make any criticisms to you personally in future. After all, if the criticism has validity, how can you be expected to act on it if you do not know what it is?

### Dealing with a Stuart

- Get him alone so he cannot play to an audience.
- Look him in the eye and ask him if he meant to be hurtful.
- If you hear something from a third party, persuade that person to tell you just what was said.
- Go back to Stuart; ask him if he really said it and whether he intended to be hurtful.
- Suggest that he voices any criticisms directly to you in future.

# Michelle

Michelle can be quite frightening to those around her. To begin with, she can seem quite pleasant and then suddenly the fuse which has been smouldering inside causes her to erupt, after which she will often lose control and start to shout, scream, curse, hurl insults – even cry with rage.

This adult version of a childish tantrum is likely to be a defence mechanism learned when very young and repeated throughout the intervening years. A combination of two circumstances is likely to cause a person like Michelle to explode. First, something has been done or said that causes her to feel personally threatened. Since this can be a chance remark to which she happens to have taken exception, there is little that can be done to avoid this happening. The second cause of an eruption is that she feels she is being put under pressure to do or say something. Because her own sense of insecurity makes her unsure of just what that action should be, she thinks that everyone else is aware of her ineptness and so she launches her attack before anyone can attack her. First she will blame anyone – or everyone – else and then she will let fly verbally.

Most people feel intimidated in the presence of this type of individual. You don't know what she is going to do next so you feel you have to treat her with caution. This means that there is no possibility of honesty or trust between you – bad enough in a work situation, disastrous when a personal relationship is involved.

You are not going to change someone like Michelle and, in an ideal world, you would have nothing at all to do with her. But this world is not ideal, so here are ways in which you can cope.

The first thing is to stand quietly, maintaining eye contact, and let her go on until she runs out of steam, which she will do eventually. Then tell her that you are keen to hear what she wants to say but not in that way. This will prove that you are taking her seriously. In order to make a break in the proceedings and allow her time to cool down, suggest that you go somewhere to talk it over – perhaps to your office, perhaps for a walk.

Having got her alone it is unlikely that the explosion will continue but, if you think she is about to begin again, interrupt before she can do so. Use her name when you speak to her and ask her to give you the details of what is troubling her. Then offer some realistic help; the help may well be refused but the fact that you made the offer will be appreciated. If there really is something you can do about the situation, tell her what it is and when you will do it – and keep your promise.

There is a certain amount of instability in the personality make-up of people like Michelle and you may find that their behaviour changes for the better just as suddenly as it changed for the worse.

### Dealing with a Michelle

- Keep eye contact but say nothing until she runs out of steam.
- Tell her you want to know what she is saying.
- Take her somewhere you can be alone, giving her time to cool down.
- Ask for details of what is troubling her.
- Offer help and, if accepted, keep your word.

# Rachel and Robert (Ponderers)

Ponderers simply cannot make up their mind what to do and so never get round to taking action of any sort. This would be bad enough in itself, but what makes it even worse is that they will promise to do what you ask – and will even genuinely mean to do so – but will never keep their promise.

There are two types of ponderers. The first (we'll call her Rachel) considers herself to be so efficient and thorough that she does not trust anyone else's capabilities. Suppose she tells you that she is too busy to look into the various types of car insurance offered and work out which is the best value for money and asks you to do this for her. You then go ahead and do as she asks. When you show her the details of your research she does not take your word but undertakes the same research all over again. But as she is so busy, the matter gets put in her 'pending' tray and she may not even get round to dealing with it before the old policy expires.

If you are faced with someone like this, you need to give her a deadline to meet – and a rational reason for doing so. With a car insurance policy the reason is fairly obvious but, if you are dealing with just one more report needed in the office, she needs to understand why it is urgent. Because she is someone who appreciates structure, she will then do what she can to meet the deadline. In addition, if you have to do some research for her, attach the results of that research to your final finding (the quotations received from all the insurance companies, for example). She may never look at them but will be happy to receive proof that you have done what you said you would.

Robert is the other type of ponderer: he is a really nice person. He wants so much to be helpful that he will promise to do anything you ask. But inwardly he is terrified either that he will do something wrong or that what he does will result in a problem for someone else. And so he does nothing at all, hoping that if he waits long enough the situation will go away – and it often does. People grow so tired of his inaction that they finally do the job themselves.

If you are faced with a pleasant, willing but useless person like Robert, try asking him to tell you what he is worried about. Suggest that he discusses his problems with you and, when he finally comes up with a solution, reassure him that you feel he is doing the right thing (if you do). He will then have the added confidence that comes from believing that the entire weight of the decision does not only rest with him but that someone else thinks he has chosen the right course of action.

Although getting the best from individuals like Robert may take added time and trouble on your part, it is often worth the effort. He really is so eager to please that, once he feels he has your support, he will work extremely hard on your behalf.

### Dealing with a Rachel

- Give her a deadline to work to and a rational reason for it.
- Attach all facts to any piece of work you give her.

### Dealing with a Robert

- Find out what he is worried about.
- Discuss problems and solutions.
- Tell him if you think he has made a wise decision.

# Daphne

Daphne is one of the most depressing people to have around. Her attitude is so negative that she pulls everyone down with her. Always anticipating the worst, her reaction to every suggestion is 'What is the point?' or 'That will never work.' Of course there are things which have no point or which won't work, but an analytical critic will follow the pessimistic prognosis with a positive suggestion (Why don't we try it this way . . .?) Daphne simply decides to be negative in advance, thus protecting herself from future disappointment. She is not going to come up with any alternative ideas; she is going to repeat as often as possible that the project is doomed to failure, although she will probably complete her tasks competently enough.

There is little point in arguing with a person like Daphne or trying to jolly her out of her negative state as she will continue to reiterate her doubts and probably drag you down to her level of despondency. It is better to acknowledge that you hear what she's saying and ask her to give you her reasons. It is a mistake to try and offer alternative solutions too quickly as she is bound to find a negative response to these too. You could put the onus on her by asking what she suggests should be done – although the answer might well be another long and negative statement.

If you were to ask a Daphne to consider the worst possible outcome of a particular course of action you would help her to analyse and express her fears, which would be far more constructive than repeatedly voicing her doubts – and, after all, this time she may have spotted a flaw in the concept that no one else has noticed. Once you have done that, however, you need to be ready to take whatever action you believe to be appropriate. Daphne's response in such a case is often 'Well, I think you're wrong but . . .' and then she will set to and offer to help.

### Dealing with a Daphne

- Don't bother to argue – it won't work.
- Avoid allowing her to drag you down.

- Ask her why she is feeling negative.
- Ask for her suggested solution to the problem.
- What are her worst fears?
- Tell her that you intend to go ahead – alone if necessary.

## George

You can always recognize George (and others like him) by his whining monotone and the way in which he links sentences with 'and' or 'but', creating one long complaining soliloquy.

George thinks everything and everyone is to blame but him – whether that means you, life, fate or luck. In his mind he sees the world as the perfect place he thinks it should be and, when it fails to live up to his expectations, he feels powerless to do anything about it. His only recourse is to seek out other people who he believes to be more capable than himself and moan to them until they do something to rectify the situation. Having complained, George thinks he has played his part and it is now up to everyone else to sort things out.

George makes life miserable for everyone with whom he comes into contact. Most people either find themselves becoming defensive or spending an inordinate amount of time trying to cheer him up so that the original situation itself is forgotten. Even when he manages to point out a real problem, his perceptiveness disappears in a morass of complaints and others tend to overlook or ignore it.

The hardest things to avoid when coping with a person like George are agreeing with him, apologizing or making excuses – but it is essential to avoid these options as they will simply prolong his moaning and whining. The sooner you can get him into a problem-solving frame of mind the better. So interrupt his flow as soon as possible and prove to him that you have been listening actively by paraphrasing what he has been saying (sticking to the point and avoiding anything that is judgemental).

Once you have stopped him in his tracks, ask him some

problem-solving questions (how? when? where? etc.). See if he has any positive suggestions to offer; he will probably react to this in one of two ways: He will either come up with a possible solution or will stare blankly, mutter 'I don't know' and go away. If the latter, he will probably go off and moan at other people and, although this is not the ideal outcome, at least it will stop him bothering you.

### Dealing with a George

- Don't agree, apologize or make excuses.
- Try and put him in a problem-solving frame of mind.
- Interrupt as soon as possible.
- Paraphrase what he has been saying (only the fair criticism, not the judgemental complaints).
- Ask problem-solving questions and see whether he can offer a positive solution.

# Sheila

Unresponsive people like Sheila hope that, if they continue to keep quiet, you will eventually stop asking them questions. When you get nothing out of them except a grunt, a silent stare or, at best, an instant change of subject, you are confused. It is impossible to fathom the reason behind their lack of response and so you end up feeling puzzled or angry.

There could be several reasons for a Sheila's reaction. Perhaps she is trying to exert power in a negative way by withholding information; perhaps she is trying to avoid an unpleasant situation (although she would never admit the fact); perhaps she is genuinely confused and does not know what to say for the best – so she says nothing. But of one thing you can be sure – Sheila always remains silent intentionally.

If you are to cope with a person like Sheila, you *must* get her to talk to you, difficult as this may be. She is not going to start the conversation so you must say something yourself. It is often easier to begin with idle comments – talk about the weather or offer her a cup of coffee. When she is, hopefully, a little more relaxed, ask an open question such as: 'What is your reaction to what I've said?' If, as is likely, she continues to be silent, you must be silent yourself. Throughout the silence, maintain open, friendly body language by looking at her (but not straight in the eye, as this will make her uncomfortable), leaning forward in your chair and unclasping your hands. This won't be easy; it will feel to you as if the silence goes on forever (it might help if you count the seconds to yourself inside your head; you will find that what seems like an eternity is probably no more than 10 or 15 seconds).

If she still says nothing and you reach a point when you can no longer stand it, *don't* continue to make conversation – this is just what she wants. Instead, comment on how ridiculous the situation is and repeat your original question, reminding her that you are waiting for her response. *Then you must be silent again*. If she starts to talk, encourage her by nodding your head or saying 'Mmm', but don't join in as she will grab any opportunity of becoming silent again.

You might feel that this particular type of person is frightened or confused. If this is so, try asking her whether she is worried about what you are going to say.

If everything fails and you cannot get any response at all from her, you have no alternative but to state firmly what action you intend to take with regard to her and then suggest a deadline by which she should come and tell you what is on her mind.

## Dealing with a Sheila

- Start a conversation, as you must get her talking.
- Begin with something trivial to put her at ease.
- Ask an open question.
- Remain silent for as long as possible – but with friendly body language.
- Don't break the silence with a fresh conversation but comment on the ridiculousness of the situation.

- If necessary, be silent again.
- If she starts to talk, don't join in the conversation.
- If you feel she is anxious, say so and ask her why.
- Tell her what you propose to do and suggest a time by which she should tell you what is bothering her.

## Eric and Marcia (Know-alls)

Eric and Marcia are both 'know-alls' – and yet they are two different types.

Eric is someone who truly believes that he knows better than everyone else and is the only one who can come up with the perfect solution every time. In fact he *is* often very thorough and efficient at work – although his personal relationships are usually disastrous as he creates resentment in those who should be closest to him. Because he is also aggressive by nature and a verbal bully, even when he is right Eric is a frustrating and aggravating person to have around. Other people tend to resist his suggestions on principle instead of giving them due consideration. However, if anyone suggests a flaw in his point of view, Eric becomes irate and may even walk out.

To deal with a person like Eric you must be sure that you have done your homework and can back up your views with facts. If you fail to do this he will simply decide that you are incompetent and will then ignore anything you might say. Show that you have been listening to what he says by paraphrasing back to him the main points of what he has been saying. Then ask him to explain further.

Because Eric tends to make snap decisions, even though they may be based on competency he may ignore essential details which could defeat his aims altogether. By asking him to explain, step by step, what action he feels should be taken you will help him to focus his mind on these details and he is likely to pick up on any flaws himself, thus he will not feel that he has been the object of criticism.

Giving advice makes someone like Eric feel superior (which he truly believes he is) and he will see as intelligent anyone who comes to seek his advice. Bearing this in mind, you can win him over to your side and help him to see you as an intelligent person (second class, of course) by suggesting that you take your problems to him. This is not being submissive because it is a deliberate strategy on your part.

If you don't consider it worth the effort or if your strategy does not work, you may have to stop and ask yourself whether you really want to stay in this job or this relationship and where it is likely to lead.

Marcia can be even more of a problem because, unlike Eric, she *thinks* she knows what she is talking about when, in fact, she does not. What she is seeking is the respect of those around her – although she does not really want to put any effort into gaining that respect.

Ideally, you should deal with a person like Marcia on her own. If you make her look small in front of others, you may find yourself with a permanent enemy on your hands. She is likely to become vindictive and may turn into an aggressor. Once you have her on her own, you can put forward your understanding of the facts while still allowing her to save face (e.g. 'I wonder whether you were thinking of last year's figures rather than the current ones').

If you find it impossible to take her to one side, you can still ask the same question but you will need to fill the ensuing silence with some other comment in order to avoid a crisis.

## Dealing with an Eric

- Be prepared by doing your own homework first.
- Listen actively and paraphrase to him what he has said; then ask for a more detailed explanation.
- Suggest that you take your problems to him.
- Weigh up whether the job or relationship is worth all the effort.

## Dealing with a Marcia

- Get her on her own if at all possible.

- Express your understanding of the facts and make a comment that allows her to save face.
- If you have to do this in front of other people, fill the silence with a comment.

# Geoff

It is hard to be angry with Geoff. He is such an agreeable person that to be unpleasant to him would be rather like kicking a friendly puppy. The trouble is, he is totally unreliable. If he arranges to meet you at noon, he might turn up at one o'clock – or he might fail to turn up at all. If he offers to complete a piece of work, it does not get done. And yet, when you see him again, he will put an arm round your shoulders, tell you how delighted he is to see you, ask you how you are and in many pleasant ways demonstrate how pleased he is to be with you.

Geoff wants so much to be liked and respected by others that he will never refuse to do anything for them. And, indeed, at the time he makes all these promises he really means to get them done; it is only subsequently that he finds he cannot. You and I know that no one is liked by everyone, and yet this is what Geoff and others like him are striving for. But the result of his behaviour is that people become irritated and annoyed with him – which just compels him to make even more promises he cannot keep.

It is often worth taking the trouble to deal with someone like Geoff because he can make a good friend or companion and a willing co-worker once he can learn to deal with the realities of a situation. He needs reassurance that you like and value him if he is to be able to communicate his feelings honestly instead of agreeing with everything you say. It often helps if you can bring in a few kind personal comments – but only if they are sincere. He will soon recognize false flattery and will be terrified by it.

If he claims to think that something is 'wonderful', tell him how glad you are that he likes it and ask him to point out anything – however small – he thinks could be improved. Emphasize that you are asking him this because you value his opinion. People like Geoff love a win/win situation and, provided they truly believe that you care about what they think, they will begin to communicate and may, indeed, come up with some valid points.

It is worth paying attention to the jokes and humour of a person like Geoff as behind them may lie clues to what he finds worrying. He tends to camouflage his real feelings behind a humorous exterior so that, should he think he has upset you, he can always claim that it was 'just a joke'.

## Dealing with a Geoff

- Reassure him that you like him and like being or working with him.
- Make some positive personal comments – but make sure they are sincere.
- Ask him to point out any flaws in a situation because you value his opinion.
- Look behind his humour for clues to his real feelings.

Obviously not everyone will fit snugly into one of these 13 categories. Some people exhibit characteristics of two or even three types depending upon the circumstances. But the coping methods given here will enable you to recognize and deal with these personalities as you come across them – even though, in many cases, you will not be able to change them from difficult into 'undifficult' people.

# CHAPTER FOUR

# Handling Conflict

In the home or in the workplace, conflict is a natural and normal part of life – indeed, life would be very boring without it. No two individuals think, act or feel in precisely the same way and, because each starts from a different point, conflict of some sort can never be eliminated completely. Problems arise when this friction is allowed to get out of hand and personalities (rather than ideas) become involved. Excessive conflict can make for a very stressful existence.

The causes of dispute can be many, but the basic one is that each person involved wants to have his own way. Perhaps the family is trying to decide where to go for this year's holiday; perhaps the members of the board are attempting to plan the organization's strategy for the coming decade. If all parties are unwilling to negotiate and compromise, conflict is sure to ensue.

The predominant reasons for discord include:

- differences in individual goals
- competitiveness – sometimes to an excessive degree
- misunderstandings or differences in perception
- lack of co-operation – real or imagined
- clashes of personality
- problems with authority
- individual frustrations
- being too eager to assume responsibility
- unwillingness to assume responsibility

- failure to comply with policies or stick to plans
- disagreements over ways to achieve agreed goals

A recent survey found that many managers and supervisors actually spend up to 25 per cent of their working time attempting to resolve conflicts – which makes it an expensive indulgence.

Conflict is not all bad. It can have positive aspects as well as negative ones. The type of dissension that can lead to positive results should be encouraged, although controlled. Such conflict may:

- reveal new aspects of an existing issue
- improve long-term communication between the individuals concerned
- generate enthusiasm or idealism
- enhance the role played by each individual
- result in a solution to a problem
- allow previously stifled emotions to be released
- encourage those involved to increase their potential and demonstrate their abilities

Ideally, negative conflicts should be avoided but, naturally, this is not always possible. If conflict cannot be avoided, efforts should be made to find the most positive resolution. Conflict becomes negative when:

- it takes people's minds away from the real issues
- it causes individuals or groups of people to become uncooperative
- those involved become frustrated and/or dissatisfied

The person who can understand conflict and what leads to it will be most capable of either preventing or resolving it. While some antagonisms should be avoided, some need dealing with so that they do not escalate until they are beyond control. Some methods for making this easier to achieve include:

1. Learning to recognize and accept the differences between individuals – their hopes, needs, personalities and backgrounds.

2. Listening actively to what other people say rather than making snap judgements.
3. Going out of your way to get to know those people with whom you often find yourself in conflict. Having worked on understanding yourself, try and understand why they behave as they do.
4. Seeing things from other people's points of view instead of always assuming that you must be right and they must be wrong.
5. Accepting that it is not possible for everyone to agree at all times. Not allowing this lack of agreement to make you feel angry, insecure or defensive.
6. Allowing the other people involved ample opportunity to say what they think – but requesting that they do it assertively rather than aggressively.
7. Once the conflict situation has been dealt with, seeing what can be learned from it.

Conflicts must be resolved in as positive a way as possible. This can usually be done in one of the following ways, each of which depends upon a real understanding of the situation at hand:

1. Pretending that dissension simply does not exist. If the matter is of little importance this method can work, as it can if the situation can be easily postponed.
2. Playing down any differences of opinion, particularly if this is a case where it is essential to maintain a harmonious relationship between those involved. This can prove satisfactory provided the situation is not one of major importance.
3. Using authority to influence the situation.
   When one of the people involved has recognizable authority over the others and this is accepted by all of them, he can influence the situation in whichever way he chooses – even bringing about an end by issuing an ultimatum. This may solve the immediate conflict but it does not do much for the relationship between the participants.
4. Compromising.
   When the two people (or two groups of people) concerned try and meet each other halfway.

5. Collaborating.

When everyone working towards a common aim (which each of them realizes is more important than the individuals involved) agrees to resolve the conflict by means of collaboration. This method takes time, effort, the desire to succeed and a certain amount of negotiating skill.

# Conflicting Personalities

Obviously where two personalities clash there is more likely to be a serious conflict situation – although with insight this can be either minimized or sometimes avoided altogether. With regard to conflict, the majority of people can be divided into one of four basic types: the Processor, the Dictator, the Empathizer or the Enthuser.

## The Processor

This is an individual with an extremely analytical mind; someone who is usually far more interested in what needs doing than in the people involved. He pays great attention to detail and likes to have all the facts at his fingertips. He is not aggressive but does like to get everything right at all times. Because he is not particularly people-orientated, he is more likely to send you a detailed memo than to initiate a conversation with you. On the plus side, he is accurate, organized and efficient; the negative aspect is that he tends to be somewhat unimaginative and may appear boring.

You can safely leave a Processor to make plans and carry them out capably, knowing that he will pay meticulous attention to detail. Facts are of the utmost importance to him whether he is giving or receiving information; he will go over a single point again and again to make sure that he has understood it perfectly. A sensible and logical person, he either hasn't got or will not use any intuitive abilities.

If you find yourself having to deal with a Processor, you will fare best if you present him with the precise logic he loves. The more facts you can give him the better he will like it – and the more he will be on your side. Not the quickest of thinkers, he likes to have things set out in front of him one step at a time so that he has the opportunity to link any new information with what he already knows or has experienced.

## The Dictator

This is someone capable of being extremely aggressive. His key word is 'I'. As his 'title' suggests, he is dictatorial in his approach. He wants things done and he wants them done *now*! He has a need to feel that he is in full command of every situation and would like to think that everyone else is the same – but he knows that they are not and this causes him to be impatient and intolerant. Because he says what he thinks without mincing words he can be hurtful to those he considers 'lesser mortals'. In fact, he has precious little time for individuals, being far more interested in results.

If you want things done, then this is your man. He is a high achiever who never doubts for a moment that he will reach his goals. The unfortunate part about it is that he alienates people on the way with his intimidating shouting, raging and supreme arrogance.

A verbal bully, the Dictator gives orders which he expects to be carried out immediately. And it goes without saying that they must be carried out in the way *he* wishes – he knows that his way is not simply the best one, it is the only one. A forceful personality and a supreme controller of others, the Dictator is competitive in every respect.

If you have to deal with a Dictator, it is important to take a factual approach (and you had better be certain that those facts are correct) and get to the crux of the matter at the earliest possible moment. He is not interested in pleasantries or idle chit-chat. However intimidated you may feel, acting in a submissive way will only cause him to think that you are weak and not worth bothering with. Being aggressive in return will not be helpful unless you can be as scathing as he can; if not, you will not win any argument or discussion.

## The Enthuser

Here is someone who has a certain amount of aggression in his nature but who is far more people-orientated than either the Processor or the Dictator. He is one of those people to whom the word 'charismatic' can be applied. He has a desperate need to be popular and appreciated – and he usually is. An energetic individual, he is initially carried along by his own enthusiasm and optimism but, although he has a great deal of energy, he does not always manage to sustain it long enough to see things through to completion.

Because his enthusiasm is genuine, it is contagious and he is able to motivate other people. Sometimes he will be quite happy to put forward ideas from the sidelines and then play a supportive role, as he does not have a particular desire for glory or public acclaim. It is far more important to him that others find him likable and, to this end, he develops a talent for successful personal relationships, being friendly, patient and charming.

When dealing with an Enthuser, you need to be enthusiastic too. This will help to maintain his energy level and he will be far more likely to stay with a project to the end. A person who speaks rapidly and sometimes loudly, it is best to let the Enthuser get on with the talking while you let your body language indicate that you understand and support his ideas.

## The Empathizer

The Empathizer is a kind, caring individual and a delight to know – provided you are not too anxious to get things done in a hurry. A real 'people person' and someone who needs to be liked, when he asks how you are he is genuinely interested in the answer. He always intends to be helpful but can be indecisive and a procrastinator. But he is so pleasant that it is very hard to be angry with him.

Although he will never make a successful leader, an Empathizer is a good person to have on your side; he is loyal and patient – and charming enough to boost your self-esteem when it begins to flag. However, when under stress he is likely to act in a submissive way which he will later regret and resent.

Even though he is not the person to take the lead in any situation, the Empathizer is good at motivating other people and encouraging them to go forward. Indeed, when he holds a strong belief or ideal he can be almost inspirational.

If you want to get the best from an Empathizer, try not to rush him. Listen actively to what he has to say and, provided you can do so with sincerity, show him that you like him.

Taking these four personalities into account, it is easy to see how conflict can arise when say, a Processor and a Dictator confront one another, or when there is a difference between an Enthuser and an Empathizer.

## Conflict and Stress

Conflict can cause those concerned to become extremely stressed. It is not easy to reduce that stress – particularly when there appears to be no resolution to the conflict in sight. If this is the case, various negative defensive reactions may present themselves in the stress victim:

- He may dig his heels in and stick adamantly to his own viewpoint, refusing to negotiate or compromise.
- He may become deliberately difficult and annoying, refusing not only to co-operate but even to take part in the discussions.
- His frustrations may turn to anger, causing him to act spitefully towards the other individuals concerned in the conflict.
- He may become extremely defensive and spend a great deal of time making excuses for his opinions and actions.

- Sometimes, because the conflict situation has caused his self-esteem to suffer dramatically, he will work harder than ever, pushing himself in an effort to regain it again.
- He may display some recognized physical symptoms of stress, such as headaches, insomnia or fatigue.
- Feeling that he can do nothing about the situation, he may become (genuinely or apparently) apathetic about the whole thing.
- If all else fails, he may depart from the scene of the conflict – either literally or mentally.

If you are the one who is to try and settle the conflict, you need to take into account all these individual reactions to the situation. The following hints may prove helpful to you:

- Whether the situation is work- or family-related, do your best to be impartial and fair at all times lest you create resentment among those concerned.
- If you feel it necessary to tackle any one individual about his attitude, don't show him up by doing it in front of everyone else.
- In the interests of fairness, try to keep the garrulous in check and encourage those who seem to be holding back to express their views.
- The expression of contradictory ideas can be a normal, lively and productive discussion and should not be repressed or curtailed in any way. But do try and diffuse the situation before it becomes over-heated.
- Remember that it is not opposing *ideas* that cause problems, but opposing *people*.

# CHAPTER FIVE

# Communicating Effectively

If we are to be able to relate well to others, it is essential that we communicate clearly and effectively, whether in business or personal life. Indeed, poor communication can make difficult people out of those who might not otherwise be – and can certainly cause those who are already problem types to become even more troublesome!

By 'communication' I mean the way in which we speak with and listen to others. When asked, most people prefer verbal communication to written – particularly when feelings are being discussed or instructions are being given. Because they are interacting with another person, they have a chance to clarify any points about which they are uncertain. They can ask relevant questions or request that something be repeated to make its meaning more clear. If a verbal explanation can be accompanied by a practical demonstration, so much the better.

It may well be beneficial to follow up a verbal communication with a written one so that the recipient has something to keep and to refer back to should the need arise. However, written communication alone is often insufficient as so many people 'speed-read' rather than really study a document. That is to say, they glance down it, taking in the important words and key-phrases but possibly overlooking some of the more detailed points which may make all the difference to the way in which they react to the document itself.

At formal meetings it is always better to ask for verbal reports.

Pieces of paper that are passed round a group are rarely read – and almost never studied.

Verbal communication is an interactive process requiring two basic skills – transmitting information and obtaining feedback. It is not sufficient simply to say what you want and then depart, assuming that it has been fully understood and digested. Insisting on feedback from the listener will ensure that the information has been received accurately and understood correctly.

Remember the game many of us played as children – it had various names but we always knew it as 'Chinese Whispers'. Several participants would stand in line and a sentence was whispered to the first one. He would whisper what he thought to be the same message to the next child and so it would continue down the line. When the last child had received the message he would say it aloud. I don't think I remember an occasion when that final sentence was identical to the one which had been whispered in the first place. (The classic one, which many people have heard, is a message which begins as 'Pass up reinforcements; we're going to advance' and ends up 'Pass up three and fourpence; we're going to a dance').

This game may cause hilarity among the children playing it but, if you are a manager giving instructions to your staff (which you would presumably like them to carry out) – and particularly if you ask one member of staff to relay your message to the others, it can be no laughing matter to find that your wishes have been distorted on the way. One or more of a variety of situations may cause a misunderstanding or breakdown in communications. It could, of course, be a result of poor transmission on the part of the speaker – perhaps you are not very articulate, talk in jargon or have an accent which the listener finds difficult to understand. The listener himself may be feeling anxious or may be distracted by things going on around him.

If A wants to communicate something to B, various elements are part of the process:

- What A thinks he says
- What A *actually* says
- What B thinks he hears

- What B *actually* hears
- What B *actually* says in reply
- What A thinks he hears B say

Because there can be a breakdown in any one of the above stages, there is tremendous scope for misunderstanding in even the simplest of communications. It is up to each of us, therefore, to do what we can to perfect both our transmitting and our listening techniques. But, even if we are not as perfect as we would like to be, the use of feedback will help to point out any lack of comprehension which can then be corrected (with further feedback to show that this has been done) before time and effort are wasted – and tempers lost.

## Transmitting the Message

There are three components to this transmission. You may be surprised to find that only 7 per cent of comprehension rests on the actual words we use. Thirteen per cent comes from our voice – its expression, intonation, etc. A massive 80 per cent results from our body language. So you can see how important it is these three methods do not send out conflicting messages. If they do, the listener will be completely confused.

If you were to meet a friend and ask him how he was feeling and his reply was: 'Well . . . er . . . all right I suppose,' spoken in a slow, hesitant way, what would you understand to be the message he was transmitting? Would you believe his *words*, which said he was 'all right,' or would you think that perhaps all was not well because of his voice and the manner in which he spoke?

Even when the speaker is transmitting a consistent message, various barriers to effective communication may be encountered. These include:

- *Poor concentration*: It may be that the listener has a short concentration span and you have forgotten to make allowances for this. On the other hand, he may at that moment be so over-stretched or have something else really important on his mind – either of which would reduce his ability to concentrate on what you are saying.

- *Low level of previous knowledge*: Perhaps he is new to the job; or it could be that you *believe* you have already told him something when in fact you have omitted to do so. Because the learning process involves not only receiving new information but being able to blend it with previous knowledge, if that previous knowledge does not exist (for whatever reason) the blending process cannot take place and therefore the listener cannot possibly learn what you are trying to teach him.

- *Anxiety or stress*: We all know how excess stress can make our minds go blank so, if the person you are addressing happens to be extremely nervous in general or if he is worried about what he thinks you are going to say to him, he will find it more difficult to absorb what you transmit.

- *Discomfort*: The listener may be suffering from physical discomfort of some kind – anything from toothache to fallen arches – and so his mind will be distracted as he contemplates his suffering and misfortune. This would naturally hamper any attempts he might make to take in what you are saying.

- *Prejudices and opinions*: We have already seen how a combination of the people and events involved in our upbringing can 'programme' us so that we follow particular patterns of thought or behaviour. The person you are speaking to will already have prejudices and fixed opinions of his own. You might want him to do something he would rather not; he could be convinced (correctly or otherwise) that he is just not capable of doing what you ask. All this would colour his receptiveness to your words.

- *Language*: If your listener is someone whose first language is not the same as your own, you will probably take great care to adapt your vocabulary to ensure that he understands. But even people from different parts of the same country can have difficulties. One person may find the accent of someone from a particular area hard to understand, or there may even be some words that mean different things in different regions. Some people speak far too quickly or have a speech impediment and this can also make it difficult for their message to be received.

If you are the person giving instructions, we can safely assume that you have a more extensive knowledge of your subject than the person to whom the instructions are being issued. You will therefore have to guard against a tendency to speak in 'technical shorthand' or jargon that is too advanced for your listener to comprehend – something he may not wish to admit to you.

- *Power of retention*: Some people are more adept than others at retaining what they hear and converting it from short-term to long-term memory. Others may only be able to absorb and understand relatively small pieces of information at once. You may be dealing with people of varying levels of intelligence as well as with those who have not had to study or commit anything to memory since leaving school – and that may have been some time ago. On the other hand, some listeners will have undergone some training in learning techniques and retention and will be able to absorb and mentally classify information at a far greater rate. All this has to be borne in mind when transmitting your message.

- *Distractions*: Of course some people are far more easily distracted than others. One person will be able to ignore all sights and sounds around him as he follows what is being said while another will be easily put off by the sound of road works (or even a telephone ringing) or the sight of someone he knows going past the window. There are mental distractions too; perhaps he is wondering how his son is getting on at the dentist or whether his daughter has done well in her recent exam.

- *Lost in thought:* If you are the speaker, observing your listener, it may seem to you that he looks totally absorbed in what you are saying that he is hanging on your every word. But one of your comments may have inspired a train of thought which he is now following with such concentration that he has lost track of the next thing you've said. Or he may be so anxious to make a good impression on you that, instead of listening actively to what you are saying, he is trying desperately to formulate his own reply.

- *Fatigue*: It is probably unwise to issue instructions of the highest importance towards the end of the working day (or just before bedtime if this is a home situation). However willing he may be, someone who is tired is not going to take in or remember your words with anything like the same accuracy as someone who is fresh and alert.
- *Advance decisions:* Because of a combination of two or more of the above possible barriers, the person to whom you are speaking may have decided in advance that he knows what you are going to say and, whether he is right or not, this will cause him to 'switch off' so that he fails to hear your actual words.

If you are convinced that you are doing all you can to send the right message and yet it still does not seem to be getting through to those you wish to receive it, try asking yourself whether one or more of the above barriers could possibly exist. If you are able to identify them, you can then set about doing something to improve the situation.

## Listening Skills

Unless you are dealing with someone with impaired hearing, there is little doubt that what you say will be heard. But will it be listened to? That is not the same thing at all. If you sit in an armchair, absorbed in your favourite magazine with the radio news on in the background, you will probably not take in much of what has been said during the course of the programme – even though, on one level, you have heard every word.

Active listening involves making sense of what the speaker is intending to transmit – and the best way of ensuring that you have done this is to give feedback. This means paraphrasing the message you have received in order to confirm that you have heard correctly and understood fully. You also have to take into account the speaker's voice and his intonation. Whether he has said 'I'll call you back' or 'Of course I love you,' accurate observation should enable you to decipher the message he was *really* sending.

On several occasions I have asked those attending my training courses in communication whether, when they felt they were receiving a contradictory message, they were more inclined to believe the words uttered or the other verbal/vocal messages they were receiving. The vast majority of people are more inclined to believe what they see or sense than what they hear. So, no matter how someone may protest that he is 'not frightened', if he is standing in a hunched position and darting his eyes from side to side he is not going to be believed!

Of course it is also possible for the visual message to reinforce the verbal one, as when someone comes towards you with a broad smile on his face and arms outstretched telling you that he is 'really pleased to see you'.

## Paraphrasing

Both sides of the communication scale benefit when paraphrasing is brought into use. It proves that the listener is receiving the message the transmitter intended to send. There can be a vast difference between what the speaker means and what you *think* he means – and paraphrasing can make this apparent before the misunderstanding is compounded. It can be used to obtain clarification of points which are unclear and is particularly useful when dealing with someone who is angry. If you paraphrase his words back to him, showing that you understand the situation, you will probably diffuse his anger and he will therefore be less irate and more co-operative.

If you are asking someone to do something and you are not completely certain that he has understood your instructions fully, ask him to paraphrase them back to you – particularly if the topic is new to him. Apart from the fact that it will give both of you peace of mind, when someone comes to realize that you always ask for this clarification, he is more likely to pay greater attention in the first place. But don't just say to him 'Do you understand?' because, if he says 'Yes', you will not be any wiser. He must prove his comprehension by paraphrasing.

Paraphrasing does not mean repeating parrot-fashion what has just been said. This is no indication of true understanding. What the listener has to do is tell you in his own words what has just been said to him, thus proving that he has understood it.

## Feedback

Feedback is important at every stage of communication and involves more than the paraphrasing already mentioned. The following examples may help illustrate this.

If you feel angry or irritated, it is unfair not to convey this information in the form of feedback. However much the other person wants to please you, how is he going to change his attitude or behaviour in the appropriate way if he does not even know there is anything wrong in the first place? And, if he repeats the irritating action or behaviour, you are likely to become even more angry and the whole situation may escalate beyond control, resulting in outbursts of rage quite disproportionate to what has been said or done. It is far better to be assertive and to say what you feel at an early stage.

If the message transmitted is not being understood, feedback should be immediate. No one minds repeating a single sentence or basic instruction but most people would be entitled to feel irritated if they had just spent 20 minutes giving details of what they required, only to find at the end of that time that the listener has not understood the first part of what was said.

Feedback can indicate your reaction to what is being said. It can be positive or negative, depending upon whether you like or dislike what the message conveys. You have the right to your own opinion – and as an assertive person you have the right to express that opinion (remembering that the other person has the right to disagree with you). If you find the message being transmitted hurtful (whether or not it is intended to be), say so – but in a positive rather than a submissive way. Let the speaker be aware of the effect his words are having upon you. Perhaps you find what is being said embarrassing or distasteful (as in the case of bad language or 'blue' jokes). Instead of blushing, pretending to enjoy something you do not or flouncing from the room, it is far better to say quietly but firmly 'I really do not like listening to such things. If you feel you want to say them, please do so at a time when I am not present.'

To be effective, feedback should always be immediate.

If you are the person giving the feedback, take care that you are never petty and do not use the occasion to express your own negative feelings – whether you have a headache or simply dislike the person speaking to you. For the feedback to be useful you must be specific, referring only to facts or events, not to how you feel about them.

Should you feel it necessary to give critical feedback, use the positive-negative-positive pattern: i.e., try to begin and end with a positive statement. For example, 'You've been very good about meeting deadlines until now [positive] so I was disappointed to find that your current piece of work was not ready on time [negative]. However, I have great faith in your ability to complete it as quickly and efficiently as possible [positive].'

Another point to remember when giving critical feedback is that, in order for it to be truly helpful, you should only deal with one point at a time. Its effect will be greatly diminished if you give a long list of grievances, as in: 'You're never on time for meals *and* you still haven't put your clothes away *and* what about the time you said . . .' The only result is likely to be an angry retaliation and perhaps the onset of a full-blown row.

True communication involves more than statement and feedback. Once you have given your feedback, allow the speaker to give his own response in turn to what you have just said. You may be surprised to find – particularly when dealing with a difficult person – that he may have completely misunderstood what you have said and your reasons for saying it. The assertive reaction in such a situation is a three-stage one:

1. Detail the problem – giving facts only, not judgements
2. Say how it makes you feel
3. Suggest a solution or ask the other person to suggest one

## Receiving Feedback

If you are the initiator of the conversation, *ask* the listener for feedback – whether positive or negative. Listen to what he says and then paraphrase it back to him to be certain that you have understood his point. Only after doing that should you give your reaction to his words. This process needs extra care if you are dealing with someone whom you know to be a difficult personality.

Identify the problem. What is it? How often does it occur? If the listener's reaction is hostile or difficult it does not necessarily mean he is negative about your words in particular. Observe how he interacts with others and you will soon discover whether or not he is a difficult person at all times.

You will find it helpful, when dealing with such a person, to plan when and how you are going to speak to him and precisely what you are going to say. Bearing his personality in mind, be prepared for him to be difficult and work out in advance how you will deal with the situation when it arises. You may even decide to rehearse the whole thing beforehand. You can do this alone or with the assistance of a friend or colleague who also knows the other person concerned. If the matter does not require your immediate attention, try visualizing the scene in advance, picturing your actions and expressions and seeing in your mind a successful outcome to the encounter.

The more difficult the person to whom you have to speak, the more essential it is that your behaviour is assertive and that you have confidence in yourself and your ability to carry it off.

- Explain the problem in as much detail as possible, restricting yourself to actual facts rather than opinion. Don't make accusations or start an argument. Remain as calm as possible the entire time.
- Ask for feedback so that you can be sure there has been no misunderstanding (bearing in mind that your listener's starting-point and programming might be different to your own).
- Say what changes you would like to see, telling the other person that you have complete confidence in his ability to bring these changes about. Be firm.

- Listen to his response and observe his reactions.
- If he has a valid objection, you may find it necessary to negotiate and compromise – this does not mean that you are being submissive or giving in, simply that you are bringing about a win/win situation.
- Ask for a commitment with regard to the action he is going to take and the timing of that action.
- Should he try, at a later date, to change that commitment – and assuming that there is no genuine cause for doing so – or if he slips back into old, bad habits, follow up with a reminder, remembering the positive-negative-positive formula.

## Active Listening

Because each of us is capable of listening to a rate of speech far greater than anyone can actually speak, our minds can easily wander from what is being said. Some people experience particular difficulty when it comes to listening actively. These include:

- Those who are bigoted, prejudiced or have fixed ideas
- People who love to be argumentative just for the sake of it
  No matter what others say, these people will always express a contradictory opinion.
- Very shy or nervous individuals
  These people are likely to be concerned more with themselves – how they are feeling, what others think of them, whether anyone is looking at them, etc.
- People with low self-esteem or very little confidence
  While appearing to listen, these people will probably be working out what to say next so that they do not appear foolish when it is their turn to speak. (If you have a poor self-image and have ever been asked to give the vote of thanks to the speaker at a formal meeting, you will know how it is possible to be so intent on finding something in the speech to mention in that vote of thanks that you actually manage to miss a great deal of it in the meantime.)

Should you be aware that you are communicating with any of the above types, explain to them how their attitude makes you feel, doing your best to empathize with them where possible, showing them that you really are on their side.

---

### How to Be an Active Listener

- Concentrate on what is being said.
- Remember that the speaker has the right to express his own thoughts and opinions whether or not you agree with them (and you also have the right to your own).
- Avoid anticipating what the other person is going to say, as this will distract you from the listening process.
- Offer feedback by paraphrasing or asking questions which indicate that you understand what has been said.
- Pay attention to the speaker's body language.

---

## Effective Speaking

This involves being able to put your point across assertively to anyone – whether or not he is a problem person. If you feel that you have difficulty in this, try considering the following:

- Are you allowing yourself to be intimidated by the attitude of the person to whom you are speaking? If so, practise some of the techniques described in Chapters 2 and 3.
- Keep an eye on the listener's facial expression and body language so that you know if he is growing impatient or 'switching off'. This way you can adjust your mode of communication accordingly.
- Be sure that any requests you make or instructions you give are as clear and concise as possible, leaving no room for doubt or misunderstanding.
- Use language which is appropriate to the listener.

- Request feedback and listen actively to it when it is forthcoming.
- Ensure that your own body language reinforces the words you speak.
- If you speak clearly and not too quickly, you will sound as though you are far wiser and completely in control of the situation.

## The 'Stuck Record' Technique

This is a very useful ploy when someone is being unpleasantly persistent and no other method of dissuading him has worked. (Perhaps when you are faced with an over-eager salesperson or someone who is becoming more interested in you personally than you would like.) The technique consists of simply repeating the same phrase over and over again, whatever the other person may say. For example:

'We are installing double-glazed windows at a house just down the road and – '

'I am really not interested, thank you.'

'We could do it for you for a special price as we're already in the neighbourhood.'

'No, thank you, I'm not interested.'

'It would add greatly to the value of your property.'

'I'm not interested' – and close the door.

By the time you have repeated the same phrase three times, the salesperson will probably have realized that you mean what you say. Of course, as an assertive person you accept the fact that he has the right to ask you to consider his offer – but you also have the right to refuse.

# Body Language

We have already learned of the importance of body language when it comes to demonstrating assertiveness. When it comes to communication, body language fulfils several functions. On the positive side, body language

- can transmit to other people our current emotional state and our attitude of mind
- reinforces the words we speak and completes the message we are sending
- can replace the verbal message completely (for example, if you ask someone 'Do you know where my book is?' and he simply shrugs his shoulders, you know perfectly well what he means)

On the more negative side, body language

- can mislead those watching us about how we feel
- can contradict the verbal message we are transmitting completely (when this happens, you will find that the other person is more likely to accept what he sees than what he hears)
- can be so confusing that no message at all is transmitted, causing problems for both parties

Now, you already know that folding your hands across your chest can be either a sign of aggressiveness or a desire to keep everyone at a distance. But, as a student on one of my recent courses pointed out, some people simply feel more comfortable with their arms folded in that way. If this applies to you, I'm afraid you have to take into account what the observer *believes* to be the visual message sent rather than your true intention. You may be feeling quite open and friendly – and your words may echo this – but this is not how it will appear to the onlooker if you stand or sit with your arms folded across your chest.

Negative body language is that which makes the transmitter appear either aggressive or submissive. Positive body language makes him appear assertive and therefore responsive to any feedback which may be offered.

---

**Aggressive body language:**
Standing with your feet apart
Jutting out your chin

---

Unwavering eye contact
Hands on hips
Pointing a finger
Leaning too near

**Submissive body language:**
Eyes permanently cast down
Drooping shoulders/slouched position
Lack of eye contact
Covering your mouth with your hand

**Assertive or responsive body language:**
Good eye contact (looking at the face as a whole rather
   than staring fixedly into the eyes)
Open gestures
A relaxed pose
Smiling or nodding as the other person speaks

Mirroring

Mirroring is a technique much favoured by those who train salespeople. While I can see that it can have some positive effects, there is a great danger that it can be overused to such an extent that it appears at best comical and at worst insulting. Also, as with the sales trick of repeating the other person's name, being on the receiving end of this technique can be extremely irritating.

The basic theory is that the more you can appear to be on the same wavelength as the person to whom you are speaking, the more likely he is to agree with (or buy from) you. So, if he crosses his legs, you cross your legs; if he stands with one hand in his pocket, you put one hand in your pocket; if he rubs the back of his neck, you rub the back of your neck . . .and so on. Training videos would have you believe that the other person will only be aware of this on a subconscious level and will not really realize what you are doing. My own view is that you would have to be extremely skilled in the technique to get away with it. If the other person were suddenly to become aware of what you were doing, he might well think you were making fun of him and refuse to have anything more to do with you.

You must make your own choice. If you feel that you can mirror someone subtly and unobtrusively, then by all means try it and gauge its effectiveness for yourself. If you have doubts about your ability to do so, it might be better to avoid trying it at all.

## Handshakes

You can learn more about someone from his handshake than you might think. You can also, if you feel so inclined, manipulate people (to a certain extent) by the way you shake hands with them.

- *The Aggressive*: Someone who likes to be in command of the situation will tend to grasp your hand so that his own is uppermost, his palm facing the ground.
- *The Submissive*: The submissive person's hand will be palm upwards, indicating that he is giving up control of the situation.
- *The Assertive*: The win/win handshake of the assertive person will result in his palm and yours being at right angles to the floor.

There are various handshake styles to take into account when learning to recognize personality types. But – one word of warning: Just as when considering effective speaking and listening you have to take the person's starting-point into account, you must do the same with his handshake. Someone who relies professionally on his hands (a musician, artist, surgeon, etc.) will probably give quite a limp handshake in order to protect them. So too will someone who has a physical problem, such as arthritis. If the handshake is a limp one, therefore, you may have to rely on other body language signs to see whether or not this really is an indication of a submissive personality.

- *The Cold Fish*: This is one of the most unpleasant – particularly if the hand really is cold to the touch. This weak, floppy handshake gives the impression of a weak, submissive character.
- *The Knuckle-crusher*: This is often used by the person (male or female) who wants to give the impression of being tough and in complete command – and it hurts!
- *The Glove*: This is when your hand is grasped between both of the other person's hands. It is usually done when the initiator wants you to think what a warm, friendly, honest person he is. However, it usually has the opposite effect and leaves you feeling suspicious and wondering what the other person wants from you.
- *The Stiff-arm*: If someone comes up to you and thrusts out his hand, keeping his arm stiff, you can be fairly certain that here is an aggressive type who intends to control you and the entire situation.
- *The Finger-shake*: This occurs when the other person does not grasp your hand but limply holds your fingers between his own fingers and thumb. This is a give-away that, whatever words he might speak, he has very little confidence in himself.

You see how people in general – and difficult people in particular – give you far more information about themselves than they think? If you can learn to read and understand these 'hidden' signs as well as the more obvious ones, you will be able to adapt your coping techniques accordingly and will be able to communicate better and achieve your desired results more quickly and easily.

# CHAPTER SIX

# Saying No

There are relatively few people who, when asked to do something by someone they know, find it easy to say no. Sometimes this is because they fear it might make them appear selfish or churlish – particularly if they don't feel able to come up with a good reason for their refusal. However, it can be essential to your well-being that you learn to say no. Allowing yourself to become over-burdened can lead to excess stress which, as everyone knows, creates its own problems.

If you are someone who has trouble saying no, then, in a work situation you might be the one to find your desk being piled high with work. In social circumstances, a person who has difficulty saying no to someone excessively persistent can be faced with even greater problems.

It is one thing to be helpful and willing to do someone a favour; it is quite another to feel that you are being taken advantage of. Some people fear that if they refuse to do what is asked of them the person doing the asking will no longer like them. (Although, if the only reason they like you is that you are a willing slave, do you really want their admiration?) Others may be concerned about the reaction of the one making the request if they refuse – will they have to cope with aggressiveness? This is less likely than you might think but, should there be an aggressive outburst, you have already learned something of how to deal with it – and you will be learning more.

Failing to say no – for whatever reason – can create its own problems in the short and long term. It is all very well remembering the old saying that 'if you want something done, you should ask a busy person' – but there are limits to what anyone can cope with. Surely a firm but polite 'no' at the outset (thus allowing time for the favour to be sought elsewhere) is better than agreeing and then finding that you can't possibly fulfil your promise. It is no virtue to deliver poor-quality work because you did not have the time to give it your full attention. You will not enhance your reputation and you will not be pleasing the person you set out to please.

Lisa is the competent and efficient secretary/personal assistant to the managing director of a small import agency. Because she *is* so competent and efficient her boss tends to keep piling her desk with work – telling her, of course, that the matter is 'urgent'. Because he does not prioritize the pieces of work, Lisa has no way of knowing which one really is most important. She is over-burdened and over-stretched, yet she still finds herself unable to say no to her boss. Why?

- She does not want to appear either inefficient or unwilling to do what is asked of her.
- She is frightened that her boss will be angry if she says she cannot do everything he asks.
- She is afraid of being demoted or, even worse, losing her job altogether.
- Like most of us, Lisa wants to be liked and appreciated.

Let's think about each of these factors in turn.

Lisa has been working for the same organization for some years now. There has been ample time for her employer to understand and appreciate her abilities. She has always worked hard and never given anyone reason to believe that she is not willing to do all that she can. Bearing these facts in mind, her boss is unlikely to take the view that she is either unwilling or unable to cope with her job.

No one actually likes to be faced with aggression or anger – particularly from someone she has to work with on a daily basis. But, provided Lisa responds assertively to her managing director's excessive demands, she will be able to control the situation in the unlikely event that he really does demonstrate anger towards her.

If there is so much work to be done and Lisa has already proved her willingness to take on as much as possible, her boss is not going to throw away the capable assistant he has or demote her to a lesser position. That would involve finding someone else and then training him so that he could do the same job – possibly less efficiently than Lisa herself.

Everyone wants to be liked and appreciated, but Lisa is far more likely to achieve this if she is honest and direct with her boss than if she struggles on, saying nothing until she collapses under the strain. By standing up for herself and drawing the situation to his attention she will gain his respect – and she may help him to realize how great are the demands he is making on her. There is, after all, a possibility that, never having done Lisa's job he does not appreciate how much time and effort it entails.

What is the probable outcome if Lisa sits back and says nothing?

The work will continue to pile up. Because Lisa is not informed which piece of work is the most urgent, deadlines could be missed. This would be likely to make her boss angry with her.

If there is no relief to the stressful situation in which she finds herself, Lisa could become ill. This could result in her having to take time off work, which might then compel her boss to find a replacement for her – either temporary or permanent.

Even if she does not actually become physically ill, the worry and anxiety Lisa experiences as the situation continues is going to destroy her quality of life.

Suppose, however, Lisa learns to be assertive and says no to her boss when he asks her to tackle yet another 'urgent' piece of work:

He will perhaps come to understand that his expectations of her are unrealistic and that he is putting her under pressure by continuing to act this way.

He will respect her honesty and will be more likely to treat her with proper consideration in the future.

Even more important is the fact that Lisa's own self-respect will increase. At present she does not think very highly of herself because on the one hand she cannot cope with all the work she is being given and on the other she does not have the courage to remedy the situation.

Her boss, having been made aware of the circumstances, will either be able to help her temporarily by prioritizing the work he has asked her to do or help her permanently by giving her an assistant.

How is Lisa to say no to the managing director in an assertive fashion so that she makes her point but they end up with a win/win situation? She must explain her position to him, stating that she has more pieces of work on her desk than she can do in the time given and asking him to tell her which, if any, have specific deadlines to be aimed for and which are the least urgent. She needs to point out that she cannot possibly add yet more work to her pile unless this new task is even more urgent than those already before her – in which case she will do it first while everything else moves one step down the ladder. At all times she should remain calm, speaking in even tones and maintaining eye contact with her boss.

There are many methods of saying no, but the only way to do so and retain your self-respect is to be assertive. Many people end up making excuses – which are often lies – in order to avoid doing something they would prefer not to do – 'Of course, I would like to take you to the airport but I'm afraid I have to attend an important meeting on that day.' This may get them out of an unwanted situation but also makes them feel petty and cowardly.

If you are dealing with a situation in your personal life – as opposed to your working life – perhaps you are afraid you will lose a friend if you say no.

Mary asks Sue if she will drive her over to see her mother who lives many miles away. Sue, quite happy to do a favour for her friend, agrees. The next time Mary wants to visit her mother, she assumes Sue will take her. Sue, who may have been perfectly willing to do the original favour, does not really want the drive to become a habit. And yet she likes Mary and does not want to lose her friendship. What should she do?

If Sue says nothing but continues to chauffeur Mary on her visits to her mother, she will soon become resentful and this resentment is likely to grow with each trip she makes. Eventually there may even be a scene in which she makes a stand and refuses to drive Mary any more. Because of the accumulated resentment she may even accuse Mary of being selfish and inconsiderate or of putting excessive strain on their friendship. If Mary has not even realized that Sue minds taking her she will be amazed by this outburst and angry at Sue's aggressive attitude.

If Sue decides to say no after the first journey, she might feel somewhat anxious as she anticipates the conversation between herself and Mary but, because resentful feelings have not been allowed to build up she will probably tackle the situation calmly and assertively, helping her friend to find another solution to her problem. She will certainly feel better about herself once she has asserted herself and made her position clear.

Mary may be taken aback by the fact that Sue has refused but she may also begin to realize that perhaps she was asking too much of her friend. She might become more considerate of her in future.

Of course it is possible that Mary will become angry and aggressive or that she will try emotionally blackmailing Sue by withdrawing her friendship. If this happens, Sue must ask herself whether Mary ever was a real friend or if she was just using her. If the relationship is a genuine one, then by remaining assertive but friendly Sue will soon be able to repair any temporary damage that may occur.

Remember that as an assertive person you always have the right to say no and should be able to do so without feeling guilty. You may choose to give an explanation for your refusal – but this is not the same thing as making an excuse. If someone you know asks you to lend him money but you would rather not do so and you say 'I would love to but I'm very hard up myself at the moment', you are lying and you will be all too aware of that fact. Not only will you feel bad about yourself for having done so, you may soon find yourself looking furtively over your shoulder whenever you go into a shop or hiding your purchases in case the person you have refused should see you and realize that you were not telling the truth.

If, however, your response to the request is 'It is my policy never to lend money to anyone', you are refusing (which is what you want to do), you are being perfectly reasonable and the person you are refusing will not feel that he is being singled out for unfair treatment.

---

## A Step-by-step Guide to Saying No

1. Ask yourself whether or not the request is a reasonable one and whether you want to accede to it or to refuse. (If you find it difficult to make up your mind, you probably want to refuse.)
2. If you feel you need further details, ask for them.
3. Should you come to the conclusion that you want to say no, do so.
4. Keep it short, giving an explanation but not a string of excuses.
5. Don't apologize. If you begin by saying 'I'm sorry but . . .' you are inviting the other person to try manipulating you by playing on your feelings of guilt.
6. Saying no does not stand alone. If you have a genuine desire to help the other person (even if you do not want to do what he has asked), listen assertively to what he has to say – and paraphrase it back to him so he realizes you are empathizing with him. Then give your reason for saying no and finally see if you can help him find another solution to his problem.

---

# Why Is It So Hard to Say No?

## Lack of Self-esteem

Many of us have been brought up to think of modesty as a virtue – and, of course, no one likes a braggart. But you have the right to be proud of yourself for the things you have achieved and the person you have become. Try and get into the habit of reminding yourself of those achievements and realize that anyone who tries to put you down is only demonstrating his own feelings of insecurity.

Write a list of things you have done of which you are proud: what are your talents and abilities? We all have them, whether you can add up a column of figures, bake a perfect sponge or have overcome your fear of the water in order to learn to swim. Make the list over a period of several days so that it is not coloured by the mood of any particular moment. Ask your friends and family what they think you do well (you may receive some pleasant surprises). Put the list where you can see it; look at it every day; read it aloud to yourself. It is not designed to make you big-headed but to improve your opinion of yourself.


## Negative Self-image

Feeling negative automatically goes hand in hand with tension and stress. And you can be sure that if you do not have confidence in yourself other people will recognize that fact, however hard you may try to hide it. Whether from the words you use, the tone of your voice or your body language you will be broadcasting your lack of confidence as clearly as if you were to advertise it on a giant hoarding. If others perceive you as someone with no self-confidence they will naturally treat you that way. This in turn will intensify those already negative feelings and thus a vicious circle will be created from which it may be difficult to escape.

Perhaps you are not certain whether you project this negative self-image or not. Think about your body language: how you do normally stand? Do you look other people in the eye or do you tend to avoid their gaze? Listen to your own voice – does it go up at the end of a sentence or is it always flat and miserable? Are there too many of the following phrases in your conversation?:

'I can't . . .'

'I'll never be able to . . .'

'I'm too nervous to . . .'

'There's no point in . . .'

Being negative is not only emotionally distressing, it can be physically upsetting, too. You are likely to suffer from such symptoms as headaches, stomach pains, insomnia, muscular tension . . .and more. Because these symptoms are depressing in themselves, they add to your feelings of negativity and so the whole situation continues to get worse – until you decide to do something positive to break the cycle.

When you are feeling positive you are much more relaxed, mentally and physically. You will be more confident in your ability to do your best. This does not necessarily mean that you will always win. You might go for a job interview only to find that someone else was better qualified than you for the position being offered. But, provided you know that you did your best and acquitted yourself well during the interview, you will have no reason to reproach yourself. You may be disappointed but your self-esteem will suffer no long-term damage.

Negativity attracts negativity and positivity attracts positivity. We have already seen how feeling (and therefore behaving) in a negative way will cause others to see you as someone with low self-esteem. Well, fortunately the opposite is also true. If you come across as a confident and positive person, that is how others will perceive and therefore react to you. Instead of that vicious circle, you will have created a benign one.

In addition to working on your thoughts and feelings, try and ensure that you appear outwardly to be confident and you will find that you will begin to believe in yourself more and more. Start by making certain that your body language is that of an assertive person. Then concentrate on the pitch of your voice and your intonation. Put positive phrases into your conversations, such as:

'I am certain that I can . . .'

'I'll do my best . . .'

'I am good at . . .'

A short time ago I asked you to make a list of your achievements. Now make another list, this time of occasions in the past when you have acted in a negative way. Take one of those occasions and write a short script for yourself explaining (in the present tense) how you'd act when feeling positive. For example:

'I have been asked several times to stand for election to the committee of an organization which raises funds for a charity I support. I have always refused.'

'I am being asked to stand for election to the committee. I accept gladly because I want to play my part in helping to support a cause in which I believe. There are several other people on this committee, so if at any point I am unsure about what to do there will always be someone happy to advise me.'

When you have written your script, pin it up so that you can see it regularly. Read it aloud to yourself. Visualize yourself in the positive situation. You will soon find that the more confident image is accepted by both your conscious and your subconscious mind.

## Guilt

Guilt is one of the most destructive of the emotions – and most of us suffer from it to a greater or lesser degree, whether it is guilt over something we have done or guilt for something we have failed to do. It's not a pleasant feeling, so when someone asks us to do something we do not want to do, we hesitate to refuse because then we might experience that horrible feeling again.

Perhaps it is worth analysing what makes you feel guilty and why it has such an effect upon you. The programming may well have started when you were a child – particularly if you had the type of parent or teacher who made you feel guilty for every misdemeanour, however minor. Of course you have made mistakes in the past – so have I and so has everyone else. We all can look back on deeds we wish we had not done or words we wish we'd never uttered. But looking back on past errors is valuable only if we learn from them. To look back in order to indulge in pangs of guilt is a dreadful waste of energy. How much better it would be to turn that energy around and use it for some beneficial purpose.

If you have something in your past about which you feel guilty, instead of trying to push it to the back of your mind (where it will do most harm), stop and study it and ask yourself a few questions:

- Do the guilty feelings arise because of some accident or a deliberate action on your part? Intention should make a great difference to the way you feel. There is a vast difference between accidentally breaking a precious ornament and deliberately hurling it against a wall – even though the final outcome is the same. If something was your fault, the only thing you can do is try and make amends in whatever way seems most appropriate, then decide not to do that same thing again in future.
- Have you changed in attitude or behaviour since the occasion about which you feel guilty? If you have – and provided the change is for the better – perhaps you should be grateful for the occasion because it has helped you to be a better person.
- Is the guilt from which you have been suffering the result of someone else's words? Some people are only too happy to relieve themselves of any blame by insisting that 'it was all your fault.' If this is the case, stop and look carefully at the situation. How much was it really your fault and how much were those words the result of some insecurity on the part of the accuser? Do you both start from the same point, so that what seems wrong to one seems wrong to the other? If not, why do you assume automatically that the other person's view was the right one?

## The Need to Be Liked

This relates back to your level of self-esteem. If you do not really like or appreciate yourself, of course you will find it gratifying to have others repeatedly telling or showing you that they like you.

Of one thing you can be certain: even if you do everything perfectly, not everyone will like you. No one is to blame for this – we are simply all different. Agreeing to everything asked of you in order to make 'everyone' like you is bound to fail. It is possible for everyone to appreciate your positive characteristics and to respect your abilities – but only if you do so first. If you don't like and appreciate yourself, no one else will. Others certainly won't be inclined to do so just because you allow yourself to be a 'dogsbody' and perform every task requested of you. Once you respect yourself you will find that you do not even mind about those people who don't really like you.

Even if you never admit the fact, other people will soon realize that the only reason you do everything they ask is that you have a desperate yearning to be liked. Those who are unscrupulous will then take advantage of this fact and heap even greater burdens upon you. We all know the type of person who will be your 'friend' provided you are happy to run around after him. But do we really want or need such 'friends'?

Saying no when it is what you want to say is your right. As an assertive person you are entitled to uphold your rights – remembering, of course, that other people are entitled to theirs, too.

# CHAPTER SEVEN

# Dealing with Complaints

No one enjoys being on the receiving end of complaints, whether it is in business or personal life. Indeed, your usual reaction is probably a negative one: you become defensive, angry or despondent. Unfortunately, such a response does nothing to ease the situation but only serves to inflame the 'complainer' further. And so the situation grows ever worse.

In many cases a certain amount of unfairness is involved. A customer or client may complain vehemently to anyone who happens to be there behind the desk or on the other end of the telephone even if that person was not responsible for whatever has gone wrong. Someone who is particularly angry is unlikely to take the time or trouble to acknowledge this fact. He simply wants something done about his grievance.

It is not easy to remain calm when you are being harangued, whether the fault is yours or not. But it is essential that you do so, for several reasons:

- If everyone becomes irate and aggressive, absolutely nothing will be achieved. The situation will become increasingly difficult and the complainer will see your attitude as something else to complain about.
- However difficult it may be, bear in mind the old adage that 'the customer is always right,' remembering that no business can exist without customers or clients. Even if he has made a mistake, the complainer obviously thinks he has a reason to feel

aggrieved and as such should be listened to. Without customers or clients, the company would collapse and you would not have a job. For these reasons it is far better to do what you can to diffuse the situation rather than join in a heated altercation.

- If the conversational temperature is not lowered, accusations are bound to go beyond the boundaries of complaint to personal comment. This would be irrelevant and unfair – but highly inflammatory and could lead to difficulties and complaints disproportionate to the original problem.

- Because it is much easier to become enraged than it is to calm down, if you allow a complainer to put you in a bad mood you are quite likely to take it out on the next poor person you have to deal with. This would not only be unfair, it would give someone else a genuine cause for complaint.

- If you allow someone to make you angry, your stress level will rise and you may find your health beginning to suffer – particularly if you are in the habit of meeting aggression with aggression. Short-term health problems such as headaches, back pain or stomach cramps are bad enough, but should the situation occur frequently enough you could well find yourself suffering from raised blood-pressure, an ulcer or – in more extreme cases – a serious heart condition.

- Another result of allowing yourself to become over- stressed is that it is impossible to contain it. In other words, if it is a situation at work which is causing the tension and you cannot retaliate to the complainer, whom are you likely to take it out on when you get home? Take your stress home with you and you will find yourself becoming angry and irritable with members of your family. Because this will be unjust they are likely to meet your aggression with angry words of their own and before you know it you have created a conflict situation. Similarly, if the original problem arises because of difficulties at home and you allow yourself to become over-stressed there and to take that feeling to the workplace with you, you will start the day in a bad mood and everything will go downhill from there.

- You know that it is no part of your job to lose your temper with a client or customer. If you find yourself doing so you will feel bad about it for the rest of the day. This is bound to affect your work and may even rub off on those colleagues with whom you come into contact.

## What to Do With a Complainer

First of all, because this is never an easy situation to deal with, make up your mind to be as relaxed as possible. Take a few deep breaths; make sure that your shoulders and jaw are as free from tension as you can make them and that you are feeling calm.

Initially you are unlikely to have any way of knowing whether the complaint is, in fact, justified, or whether the complainer has somehow misunderstood the situation or just enjoys complaining for its own sake. So you should always begin in the same way. Let the complainer – particularly if he is showing signs of aggression – let off steam until he slows down and comes to a stop (as he will have to do eventually). If you fail to do this but try to interrupt in order to put your side of the story or to give an explanation, he will simply take a deep breath and start all over again.

Whatever happens, and however irate the complainer may become, be sure that you keep your own temper. Speak to him in a friendly, helpful tone. If you lose your temper it will help no one and solve no problems. Your body language should be assertive, so maintain eye contact; lean slightly towards him in an open manner.

Listen actively and let him see that you are doing so. You might wish to take notes to ensure that you have understood all the facts correctly. Not only will this help the complainer to see that you are taking the matter seriously, it stops you jumping to any wrong conclusions or making assumptions before you have heard the whole story.

Having listened to what he has to say, show the complainer that you empathize by giving him positive feedback. Paraphrase what he has been saying to you and include a phrase or sentence showing that you understand why he is so upset. For example:

'I understand how angry you must be that the delivery has been delayed for the third time.'

This will help to show him that you are sympathetic and that you do not think he is acting unreasonably.

Of course you must at some point look into the matter in detail. You cannot always assume that the complainer is correct and the company in the wrong – although in some cases this will be obvious. Offer to look into it for him and if it is something you cannot do there and then tell him this and let him know when you will get back to him. *And make sure that you do so.*

If it is immediately obvious that the organization has made a mistake, or if you discover this as a result of your investigations, admit it and apologize. There is no point in trying to cover up an error or pretend that it never happened; you will simply alienate the complainer even more.

Never start making excuses ('It's not my fault,' 'I wasn't the one who dealt with this,' 'We've had a lot of problems lately,' etc.). At this point the complainer really doesn't care whose fault it is; from his viewpoint, you represent the company. If you tell him that there have been a lot of problems lately he may well lose faith in the company altogether and valuable business may be lost as a result. Never waste time defending yourself or laying the blame on someone else. It is not relevant and the complainer will not be willing to listen. The important thing is to do what you can (and to be seen to be doing so) to put the matter right.

Once you have ascertained the facts behind the complaint, explain what you are going to do – and do it.

Even a normally mild-mannered person can become quite aggressive when he turns into a complainer – especially if this is not the first time something has gone wrong. It will not be possible to sort out the facts of the matter and begin to solve the problem until you have dealt with his feelings. Make it clear that you understand his position and empathize with him. Even if you feel that he is making a mountain out of a molehill, keep calm and don't allow yourself to react negatively. Let him talk, as this will usually diminish his aggression (especially if he is able to see you taking notes and writing down all the relevant facts). Listen to him, nodding your head a little as he talks and, when it is your turn to speak, do so calmly and slowly, repeating the facts to him so that he realizes you have fully understood the situation.

Only then can you turn to dealing with the problem itself. The most important thing is to ask the complainer what he would like you to do. 'I understand the problem; how would you like me to help you?' This is essential because different people may want different things – and some really only need an opportunity to let off steam. Interestingly, however long the complainer has gone on, when asked directly he may find that he does not really know what he wants you to do.

Even if the complainer knows exactly what outcome he would like, sometimes it will not be possible for you to do just as he wants. If this applies, tell him and offer the nearest alternative. It is quite a good idea to proffer two suggestions and ask him which one he would prefer. It makes him think that he is once more in charge of the situation.

Perhaps the mistake will actually be yours. If so, the only thing to do is admit it, apologize and ask what you can do to put it right. Don't bother to make excuses – 'I've been run off my feet . . . my assistant has been away for a week . . . I have had a terrible headache . . .' This will merely make you appear weak and ineffective. Unless the complainer is a particularly difficult person (in which case nothing is going to satisfy him), he will understand and accept that all human beings make mistakes. He is more likely to respond positively to an honest admission and a desire to put things right than to a long list of excuses which he may or may not believe.

If it really is impossible to rectify the matter in the way that he wants, you may need to employ the 'broken record' technique. For example, 'I do understand but I can't make any exceptions'; it may not be what the complainer wants to hear and, in fact, initially he may not hear it but continue ranting at you. If necessary you can calmly and quietly repeat the same phrase several times until it eventually sinks in. *Then* see if you can find another solution.

If the complainer is obviously a really difficult person who is looking for an argument, don't allow yourself to react aggressively in return. This doesn't mean, however, that you should be either defensive or submissive. This would only make him try to enhance his own opinion of himself by becoming even more aggressive. Even if you feel that the complaint is completely unjustified, see if it is possible to find any area of agreement. This will make it very hard for the complainer to continue his aggressive stance – how can you shout and scream at someone who is agreeing with you?

Should it really be completely beyond your scope to find a solution to the problem, try to postpone action in order to have time to find out more about what needs to be done. Tell him that you will get back to him as soon as possible – making sure, of course, that you then do so.

---

### Checklist for Handling Complaints

- As soon as you realize that you are about to be faced with a complaint, take a few deep breaths and relax as much as you are able.
- Whatever happens and whatever the attitude of the other person, be sure that you stay calm and that your tone of voice and your body language indicate that you are being assertive and are not intimidated by him.
- Empathize with the complainer. Try and see things from his point of view. Make it clear to him that you understand his feelings and the reason for them.
- Listen actively, taking notes if appropriate. Confirm that you have the facts straight by paraphrasing what the complainer has said. If you feel that you haven't sufficient information to deal with the problem, ask for more details.
- Keep to the point. If the complainer wanders away from the topic under discussion, gently but firmly bring him back to it. Make sure you are both dealing with the problem at hand and that personalities are not allowed to become the issue.

---

- Having listened to what he has to say, ask him what outcome he would like to see.
- Offer a solution – the one he wants if this is possible. If not, suggest one – or preferably two – alternatives and ask which he would prefer. Negotiate a compromise if necessary, doing your best to create a win/win situation.

Mr Smith of F.S. Manufacturing recently ordered 5,000 super-widgets from The Amalgamated Widget Co. However, when the delivery arrived, it was found to contain 5,000 *standard* widgets. Mr Smith originally telephoned to report this fact; he received an apology and the promise of an immediate replacement. When the next delivery arrived, however, it was found to contain a further 5,000 standard widgets. A furious Mr Smith has now arrived at the Parts Department where he is met by Peter, who has recently joined the company. Before Peter can say a word, Mr Smith launches an attack, pounding the counter-top and shouting as he calls the company, the department and even poor Peter every name he can think of.

Peter lets him continue until he runs out of steam and then, taking a couple of deep breaths, starts to speak:

*Peter*: Mr Smith, I do understand how irritating all this has been for you. Let me see what I can do to help you.

*Smith*: Irritating – it's more than irritating! Because of your company's stupid mistake, we're having to hold up production.

*Peter*: I realize that makes things very difficult for you, so I am going to get this matter sorted out today. Perhaps you could give me more details – order number, dates and so on – so that I can check with the delivery department right now.

(Smith provides the relevant details, which Peter writes down. He then double-checks them with Smith to ensure he has noted them correctly.)

*Peter*: Now, there are two ways of handling this: I can have 5,000 super-widgets sent over here immediately and you can take them away with you or you can go back to your company and I will arrange for the super-widgets to be delivered there this afternoon. Which would you prefer?

*Smith*: I need those widgets right now but the vehicle I've come in isn't large enough to take 5,000.

*Peter*: Well, why don't you take as many as you can – say, 2,000 – in your vehicle and I will make absolutely certain that the remaining 3,000 reach you before the end of the working day.

*Smith*: I suppose that seems fair enough.

*Peter*: And, Mr Smith, I do apologize for the trouble you've had and I can assure you that it will not happen again.

## Telephone Complaints

Particularly in the world of business, complaints often reach you by telephone, which can cause further problems:

- Some people who might not normally act aggressively find it easier to do so when speaking to a faceless voice at the other end of the line.
- Because they have already spoken to a receptionist or switchboard operator who has then had to transfer the call to you, they have had more time to become even more irritable. If the receptionist is not particularly efficient and has either taken too long to connect him or has initially put him through to the wrong person, the complainer is likely to be near exploding-point.
- Many people, particularly if heated, become far less coherent on the telephone than they would be if you were dealing with them face-to-face. You will therefore have more difficulty establishing the facts of the case.
- You cannot see his body language (which, you will remember, is responsible for about 80 per cent of our understanding) and of course he will not be able to see yours, so until you speak

he will not know whether you are being assertive, whether he has cowed you into submission or whether you intend to retaliate with aggression of your own. If he is in a bad mood he is most likely to assume that the last will be the case and so may become even more aggressive than he would otherwise be.

Because of the problems listed above, it is even more important than usual that you remain calm and polite when dealing with a telephone complaint. Even if the call is responsible for interrupting other work, don't allow yourself to show *any* irritation. This is not always easy – particularly as you may find that, in the beginning, the complainer is not really listening to what you are saying, being so engrossed in his own grievances.

Keep a pen and pad by your telephone at all times. Once the complainer has slowed down, interrupt and ask for his own name and, if relevant, that of his company – asking him to spell it if you are unsure. If you have to leave the telephone at any time (to find an appropriate document or check something on the computer), ask him if he wants to hold on or if he would prefer you to call him back.

Never put your hand over the mouthpiece of the telephone while speaking to someone else. For one thing, the complainer (especially if in a bad mood) will automatically assume that you are being rude about him. For another, it doesn't work! The way most modern telephone handsets are constructed, the sound travels just as well through the holes in the earpiece as in the mouthpiece.

If you need to interrupt the complainer, always do so by using his name. 'Mr Jones' is more likely to make him stop and listen than 'Excuse me . . . but . . . I just . . .'

Take a note of any details and then paraphrase them back to him just as you would if he were standing before you. If you can deal with it yourself, tell him so and explain what you intend to do – giving him choices if appropriate.

If it is something you cannot handle there and then, promise you will call him back, telling him when you will do so and giving him your name so that he knows whom to speak to should he need to ring again. Of course, you will make sure that you do phone him at the right time even if it is only to give a progress report because the matter has not yet been sorted out completely.

If you cannot deal with it personally, tell him this and assure him that you will contact the relevant person and that that person will telephone him to discuss it. You will then have to check that this has been done.

# CHAPTER EIGHT

# Coping with Authority

No matter who you are, how old you are or what your situation may be, there is someone who is in a position of authority over you. It may be a parent, a teacher, a supervisor, the police or a government department – there is always someone there with the power to tell you what to do. Difficulties arise when the people with power are not capable of using it effectively in order to get the best from those around them.

Whether you are the supervisor or the supervised, your attitude towards authority has been predetermined by the first authority figures with whom you came into contact. These are likely to have been your parents (or those who stood in that position) or teachers. The way these people acted towards you and the way you responded to them will have greatly influenced the person you are today.

A small child will always believe that his parents are all-knowing, wonderful beings who never make mistakes. So, should one of those parents be severely over-critical, he will take those criticisms to heart. After all, how could such wonderful people be wrong? And unless at some point he actively sets about changing that original self-image, he will grow up to believe himself worthy of criticism and will therefore accept it throughout his life.

If you feel that you have such an attitude, perhaps it is worth looking back in your life and asking yourself whether you were belittled or repeatedly criticized when you were young. It could have been anything from being constantly told that you were 'hopeless' or 'stupid' to being compared unfavourably with brothers, sisters or classmates. Should you feel that this (or something similar) applied to you, ask yourself whether the attitude and words of an insensitive person should continue to have such a devastating effect on you or whether you are prepared to work at doing something to change the situation.

The dominant early authority figure does not have to have been uncaring. Perhaps you were greatly loved but over-protected as a child, with everyone doing everything for you. This could have caused you to feel that you were incapable of dealing with problems for yourself and therefore left you with an inability to stand on your own two feet now you are adult.

Your development may have been hindered because someone else liked to be seen as the 'clever' one and therefore never gave you the opportunity to show what you could do. Whatever the reason for your sensitivity to authority, you can do something about it. You cannot change what has happened in the past but you have control over your future.

## Aggressive Authority Figures

No one has the right to be aggressive towards another person (except perhaps when faced with physical aggression from someone else – in which case it might be necessary). Aggressive behaviour, particularly from someone who is already in a position of authority, is usually a way of dominating others rather than leading them. The aggressor wants to *compel* others to do his bidding – although he would get far better results by *asking* them.

If you are faced with authority that is difficult in any way, do take into account that we are all human beings with human faults and failings. Try not to jump to negative conclusions if difficult behaviour occurs only rarely. It is only when such behaviour is the norm that it constitutes a problem and needs to be dealt with using some of the assertive techniques mentioned here.

## Are You Being Kept 'in Your Place'?

You may be an over-protected child, someone who is treated as the 'little wife' or stymied in your progress at work. The latter two are often the result of someone else wanting to appear more important than you are; in order to achieve this he has to hold you back, thinking that this enhances his own standing. Whatever the reason, the result is that your personal development is stifled and that a sense of resentment builds up in you towards the person who is preventing you from making progress.

In such a case the only thing to do is act in an assertive manner. The matter needs to be brought into the open and you will have to discuss the problem with the authority figure who is holding you back. You will, of course, have to choose your time carefully. There is no point in broaching the matter when the other person is in a bad mood, as nothing will be achieved. It is also a good idea, particularly if you are not used to speaking out, to work out in advance what you want to say. Your script should cover the following points:

* the present situation
* how it makes you feel
* what you would like changed
* what the result would be

An example of this four-point plan might be:

'Every time I start to fit a plug to an electrical appliance, you take the screwdriver out of my hands and do the job for me' [the present situation];

'This makes me feel inadequate and that you look upon me as someone who is incompetent; I find that hurtful' [how you feel];

'Please allow me to get on with the task myself' [the change you'd like];

'In that way I can save you the trouble and give you more time to do other things' [result].

## Do You Never Receive Recognition?

Whatever you do, your authority figure never praises you and yet he is all too ready to criticize you if he feels you have done something wrong. Some people think that such an attitude will act as a spur and drive you on to greater and better things – but this is rarely the case. More often the person being constantly criticized simply gives up trying. This may be because he has become extremely (and understandably) resentful of this lack of appreciation or because he believes that, if he is going to be criticized anyway, there is little point in bothering to continue with the task he was performing.

Of course, it is possible that your severe critic is insensitive enough not to realize the effect his attitude has upon you – in which case he will have to be told. But it is even more likely that he feels that to praise you would make him seem less wonderful than he would like to believe himself to be.

The solution in this case is to explain how his treatment makes you feel and to point out to him that everyone likes to be appreciated and is able to respond more to positive than to negative feedback.

Do remember, however, that if he makes the effort to change and begins to acknowledge your achievements, you must not spoil things by being bad at accepting these compliments. It may take some effort on his part to change his ways and, should he be knocked back by a negative response from you, he is unlikely to try again.

# Verbal Aggression

Although we tend to think of aggression as being synonymous with shouting or other displays of bad temper, there are, in fact, many forms of verbal aggression which can be used by those who are in a position of authority in order to achieve what they perceive to be their aims.

## Sarcasm

It is not for nothing that sarcasm is called 'the lowest form of wit'. It is designed to belittle and to hurt the recipient – usually in front of others so that the aggressor's opinion of himself is bolstered by the (sometimes awkward or embarrassed) laughter or appreciation of others. To some extent those who hear sarcastic remarks directed at a colleague and allow themselves to join in the laughter are also being aggressive – although the cause may be partly one of relief that they themselves are not the victims.

Sarcasm is aggressive because it is used in order to make another person toe the line and do what the aggressor wants him to do. Only someone who is inwardly insecure will actually use sarcasm to achieve these ends; anyone who respects himself and others does not need to stoop to such a level. Just as the physical bully is really a coward and full of self-doubt, so too is the person who repeatedly tries to get his way by use of sarcasm. And, just like the person being bullied, the more the unfortunate victim responds and reacts to the sarcasm, the longer the torment will continue. There are two ways in which you can deal with sarcasm:

1. Do nothing. Don't allow yourself to react in any way at all. Just sit quietly and get on with what you are doing. This will confuse the sarcastic person, who *wants* a reaction from you – whether you become upset, angry, tearful or distressed. He does not really know how to cope when things are not going his way. Unfortunately it will not change his nature – only he can do that – but it will make him stop picking on you and direct his sarcasm elsewhere.
2. If you feel either that you cannot remain impassive or that you would prefer to respond to the sarcasm, be assertive and tell the perpetrator how you feel. For example, 'That was a sarcastic remark; why did you feel you had to say it?' Or, 'I find your sarcasm really hurtful; did you intend it to be?'

If, as is probable, the aggressive person knows perfectly well that his sarcasm is hurtful, he will be taken by surprise by your response and will not know what to say. He may begin to bluster or he may try and make excuses. Either way, he will be showing himself up in the eyes of the onlookers – which is the last thing he wants – and realizing that you are now in control of the situation, he will soon stop.

But suppose for a moment that we give the sarcastic person the benefit of the doubt and assume that he does *not* realize how much distress his so-called wit causes. In this case your comments will draw this to his attention and may make him more careful in future about the way in which he chooses his words.

## Criticism

Criticism in front of others is never really justified. Whether we are talking about the manager in the office, the teacher in the classroom or the nagging husband or wife, if one person feels the need to criticize another it is best done in private where only the people concerned are present. Of course there are occasions when criticism is justified – but there are still assertive (rather than aggressive) ways of using it. Assertive criticism always involves giving an explanation of the situation as the critic sees it, stating why it is a problem, how it makes him feel and describing what he wants to see done about it.

If you are criticized in front of other people, here is a two-stage response which should prove effective.

1. Because it will only aggravate the situation if you immediately stand up and proclaim 'I think we should discuss this in private,' it is simpler, on the first occasion, to concentrate on responding to the fairness or otherwise of the criticism. If it is justified, all you can do is accept that fact and state what you intend to do to rectify the situation. If you feel that the criticism is unfair, you must say so calmly and assertively and give your interpretation of events.
2. The second stage should take place at an appropriate moment as soon after the criticism as possible but not while you can see

that the critic is still in an aggressive mood. When the time appears right, approach the critic and ask if you can speak to him in private. If he says he is busy, ask when would be a suitable time. At that time you should explain to him that, even when what he has to say is justified, you find it hurtful and demeaning to be criticized in front of others and would be happier if in future he would do so in private.

To be effective, fair criticism should *never* involve being judgemental about the personality of the person being criticized. For example, if a supervisor says 'You've made three mistakes in this report – you're stupid!' only the first part is fair criticism. 'You're stupid' is a character judgement which is irrelevant and aggressive – and which you do not need to answer. It is important that you do not allow yourself to react to such judgemental remarks, as eventually judgement leads to labelling – and this can be very difficult to shift. For example, 'Henry's always late,' 'Jane's such a little mouse' or 'Don't give it to Fiona – she's so clumsy that she's bound to drop it.'

## Rages

Some people make a habit of flying into a rage. They seem incapable of expressing themselves without screaming, shouting, banging the table, slamming the door – or, in some cases, throwing whatever is to hand. If you are in the firing line these rages can be extremely difficult to cope with – and for someone with a meek, submissive personality, they can prove impossible.

Such displays of temper indicate loss of control in the aggressor and this in turn is a sign of immaturity, whatever his actual age may be. Perhaps as a child he found that throwing a tantrum was the best way to manipulate his parents and so he continues to use a similar method today. Perhaps he came from a family where it was the person whose voice was loudest or who was able to be the most disruptive who got his own way. Whatever the original reason, anyone who regularly flies into a rage will have seen it get results from a very early age and so determines to continue using the method to achieve his ends.

Although it is impossible to generalize, someone who indulges in temper tantrums falls basically into one of two categories:

1. The person who is always ill-tempered, never having learned that it is in fact easier to get what you want by being pleasantly assertive than by trying to force others to co-operate.
2. The highly-strung individual who is just as extreme when displaying any emotion. This person probably does not like himself very much when he loses control of his temper but does not know how to go about changing the situation. However, because he usually is also able to laugh at himself once the moment has passed, he is easier to deal with than someone in the first category.

If you are confronted by the first type of tantrum-thrower, the one who is always dissatisfied and whose humour never really improves, the rages will be very difficult to cope with. There is never going to be a moment when you can discuss the situation with him because there will never be a time when he will be prepared to listen – particularly to anything which may be a criticism of him or his behaviour. One thing such an aggressor cannot cope with is any intimation that he might be wrong about something or that his behaviour may be less than perfect. He is only capable of seeing things from one point of view – his! Of course, this is another sign of immaturity and weakness, as a strong person is quite able to recognize and admit his own shortcomings. In this case, you have to accept that you are never going to change him, so here are a few methods of self-protection you can employ:

• Try not to take his comments or his attitude personally. Realize that he is just as unreasonable towards everyone else and that his remarks are not aimed solely at you. If you can keep this thought in mind, hopefully his behaviour will be less distressing and you will be more able to sit back and wait for the storm to pass.

- Make a joke of it inside your head. He is behaving childishly so imagine him as a child. As he rants and raves, imagine that he is wearing a school cap and short trousers – or even a nappy. It will put the matter more in proportion in your mind, even though it will not change his behaviour.
- If you find yourself becoming really upset and there is nothing you can do to stem the flow of his temper, see if you can remove yourself from the scene. But don't run out of the room showing obvious signs of distress – this will only make him feel contempt for what he sees as your 'weakness' and so he will have something more to shout about. The assertive reaction would be to say something like, 'I am not prepared to stay here and be treated in this way; I'll be back when things are calmer' or 'I find it upsetting when you shout and throw things so I would be grateful if you would stop. Until then I shall find things to do elsewhere.' If you find saying either of these things really difficult, all you have to do is stand up and quietly say 'Excuse me' and then walk away – if possible, out of the room.

If you are dealing with the second type of person, the one who is extreme in all his behaviour, you will find that there are times when he is not in a rage and is quite approachable. Pick one of these times and ask if you can have a quiet word with him. Then you can continue by explaining to him how his outbursts of rage make you feel and the effect they have on you and others. For example, 'You know, when you fly off the handle like that it really makes things difficult for all of us. I find it quite distressing and Sally is becoming very upset and her confidence is ebbing every day. It also makes it almost impossible to understand what you are trying to say – so we can't comply with your wishes however much we want to.'

You will probably find that, when forced to look at himself and his behaviour, this type will be full of remorse. He may be quite generous with his apologies and he will mean them sincerely. A further problem may arise because, like so many other things, tantrums are a habit and he may find himself reacting in a similar way on the next occasion. To prevent this happening, tell him that you realize he probably loses his temper without consciously thinking about it and that it will be a difficult habit to break. Ask if he'd be willing for you to help him by giving him a signal should he begin to rage again. If he acquiesces, agree on an appropriate signal between you.

If your relationship warrants it, try and inject a little humour into the situation. A delegate attending one of my seminars told how she 'cured' her supervisor of his outbursts of temper. (Though you need to bear in mind that her office had a relatively easy-going system; the same thing might not be possible in a more formal atmosphere.) The delegate (I'll call her Caroline) had just witnessed another example of her supervisor's fiery temper in the office. About 10 minutes after it was all over, she held a heavy file in front of her like a shield and peeped round the supervisor's door. 'Is it safe to come in now?' she asked. He looked puzzled, being one of those people whose bad temper completely disappears once the rage of the moment has passed. 'Well,' she said, 'you were in such a rage just now that I thought you might still be throwing things. I brought the file in with me to protect myself.'

The supervisor smiled a little awkwardly. 'I suppose I did get into a state,' he said. 'But take no notice – it's all over now.' Caroline went into the room. 'If you're not going to throw the fax machine at me, could I have a word with you?' He nodded and she sat down. Then, in a calm but assertive way she explained to him the effect of his rages on her and on the others in the office. Keeping her manner light, she ended by asking him if he was about to start yelling again – for, if he was, she intended to hide under the desk. The conversation concluded with both of them in good humour and the supervisor saying that he would try to curb his temper in future.

Of course, even the best intentions waver from time to time, but in this case the door to change had been opened. The next time Caroline sensed that her supervisor's temper was beginning to build, she picked up a plant in a heavy pot and handed it to him. 'In case you feel like throwing it,' she said. This brought him up sharply and he began to laugh, realizing how he was behaving. He went on to make his points in a calmer, although still firm manner. Over a period of time, he lost his temper less and less frequently.

So, if you think the authority figure you have to deal with would respond to a little gentle teasing, this can often be an effective way of diffusing potentially explosive situations.

## Silence

Refusing to discuss matters of importance – or even refusing to speak at all, can itself be considered aggressive behaviour. Obviously silence helps no one; if there is a problem, silence does nothing to overcome it; if there is a tense atmosphere, silence does nothing to relieve it. Not only this, but silence destroys any team (or family) feeling – sometimes for ever. People who sulk or avoid discussion of any kind rarely act in this way on only the odd occasion; it tends to be a regular behaviour pattern unless and until they decide to make deliberate efforts to change it. Therefore it is likely that the atmosphere in the home, office or other environment will often be tense and uncomfortable. If it is a business situation, this may lead to people requesting transfers or even changing jobs; in a home environment it can lead to misunderstandings and the destruction of all true family feeling.

Often, when these silent aggressors do eventually speak, it is to snap at those around them. Such behaviour is a sign of insecurity – which may or may not be justified. They may fear that their authority is being questioned or that someone is after their job; they may feel that they have got where they are on false pretences and that one day someone will discover how little they really know. This in no way excuses their behaviour but perhaps goes a little way towards explaining it.

If their attitude is the same towards each member of the staff or each person in the family, it is important that you try not to take it as though it were aimed at you personally. To do so could cause you to underestimate yourself in the future and to have a lower self-esteem than you should. However, it is still important that the matter is dealt with and the aggressive person approached in an assertive manner and told how his behaviour causes everyone else to feel.

Sometimes, of course, such behaviour will only be shown towards one particular person in the group and everyone else will be treated fairly. If you are the person in question, for your own peace of mind you *must* take steps to establish the cause as soon as possible. (Or if, as sometimes happens, you are a parent and you feel that the aggressor's tactic is directed towards one of your children who may be too young to speak for himself, you must do so on his behalf.)

Don't approach the aggressor in a belligerent mood; find a quiet time and ask him whether he realizes that he behaves differently towards you than he does to everyone else. If necessary, go on and explain in what way his attitude towards you is different. Try to make statements rather than accusations – however hurt you may feel. Ask him to tell you whether you have done anything to cause him to act in this way – for if you don't know what you are supposed to have done, how can you begin to make changes?

This is quite likely to be a difficult discussion because someone who uses silence as a weapon is going to find it difficult to explain his feelings. But do persevere. After you have asked a question, don't be tempted to elaborate but try to leave a long silence which he will eventually have to fill. Remain calm and assertive the whole time. Eventually you are likely to be faced with one of three reactions:

1. He may come up with a reason which is (in whole or in part) justified; perhaps he thinks you have said something behind his back or feels that you are not pulling your weight. If this is the case you can deal with the situation by explaining the truth (or apologizing if there is anything to apologize for). You can then say that you hope this will be an end to the matter and that in future you can be treated in the same way as everyone else. You can also ask that, should he feel such displeasure in the future, he should confront you rather than single you out for silent treatment.
2. He may have been harbouring some grievance for a long time, having misread an earlier situation. Possibly there has been

something in your own attitude that he has misunderstood and, because he has a tendency to be insecure in the first place, he has done everything he can to shut you out in order to avoid feeling threatened.

3. There may be no real reason for his behaviour other than the fact that he is someone who always needs to have a 'victim' on whom to pick or that he either does not like you or feels that you do not like him – and none of us can honestly state that we like *everyone* with whom we come into contact.

In any of these cases he is likely to waver, deny his behaviour or refuse to discuss the matter at all. If this is the reaction with which you are faced, you must continue to speak. Explain that you find his behaviour hurtful, especially as he seems unable to justify it and cannot tell you of anything you have done wrong. Request that, even if he feels there is little rapport between the two of you, each of you deserves the same courtesy as would be shown to anyone else.


## Put-downs

Belittling remarks can be extremely hurtful, particularly when they are made in front of other people and especially if they are of a personal nature. We have already seen that genuine criticism is valid provided it is justified, but attempts to make the other person feel small are not – and never can be.

The first thing you need to obtain is clarification of what has been said and the reason, if there is one, for the remarks. Suppose you have been told, as a young man called Martin was, that you have 'an attitude problem' – what precisely does that mean? You have to have more details. It might simply be that, because of a difference in age or personality type you do not see eye-to-eye with the person who made the comment – but that does not entitle him to put you down or belittle you. Of course, there could be a real area of conflict or misunderstanding between you but, in that case, you are entitled to be told how the situation appears to him and also to be given a chance to explain your side of the matter.

So, bearing in mind what you have learned from Chapter 2 on being more assertive, approach the person concerned and ask him why he made the remark, whether he has an area of disagreement with you and how he feels the matter could be rectified. Point out at the same time that the way in which he made his comments was not only unproductive but was hurtful to you and ask that, should he feel that there is a problem at any time in the future, he should speak to you in private explaining precisely what he wants.

If he is unable to give any valid reason for his comments – and particularly if he begins to falter or become more aggressive – then you can be fairly sure that there is no reason for his behaviour other than his own 'attitude problem'. Once you realize this, even if you cannot change the way in which he speaks and acts, his words and actions will have a far less damaging effect upon you.

If all else fails, you could try stating what the consequences will be if he continues to act towards you in such a way – whether you intend to make a written complaint or speak to *his* supervisor or department head. This remedy should only be used as a last resort when you have tried everything else you can think of. If you use it too early or too frequently, not only will you sound as though you are being vindictive but it will not have as great an impact.

Here is the way to go about complaining to someone's superior:

- First ask yourself if you have tried every other way you can think of to remedy the situation;
- Consider whether an effective course of action exists and decide whether you feel that you are prepared to use it;
- Indicate what the outcome will be if he doesn't change his attitude and behaviour;
- Be very careful not to sink to the aggressive level. What you say will only be effective if you can remain assertive (and remember that this includes your body language as well as the words you use).

117

# The Disorganized Authority Figure

It is extremely difficult to live or work with someone who makes vague requests or who gives instructions and then proceeds to countermand them. Everyone becomes confused and no one ever knows precisely where he stands, which can be quite unnerving. Using your best communication techniques, try giving this kind of authority figure instant feedback by paraphrasing back to him what he has said so that you are both quite clear as to where you stand. Even better is to write the instructions down and then show them to him and ask him to confirm that they are correct. Then, should he change his mind, you will have written proof of his original request to show him. If he is someone who unknowingly frequently changes his mind, this written proof will help him to realize what he has been doing and hopefully encourage him to become more organized in the future.

# Conflicting Authority Figures

It is unfair and confusing to countermand someone else's instructions – but, unfortunately, there are many people who do it. Whether it is in the home situation (and clever children soon learn whom to approach first – mother or father) or in the workplace (as when a manager usurps the authority of a team leader by countermanding whatever he has said) such behaviour is an insult to the giver of the original instructions and disturbing to everyone else.

If you are faced by two (or more) such conflicting authorities, the most effective way of dealing with the situation is to be completely honest with both parties and state what each has said, asking them both (at the same time and together, if you can manage it) to let you know which path you are supposed to follow. If nothing else, this will help to bring to the attention of the one that the other is countermanding instructions he has given.

# Non-supportive Authority Figures

Some superiors will always back up outsiders in cases of conflict when they should really remain neutral until they have heard both sides (i.e. that of their subordinate and that of the other person), after which they will be in a position to make a reasoned judgement.

Because of her poor payment record, it had been decided that Mrs Jefferson was not to be granted credit in the future but must pay in advance for goods ordered. This had been explained clearly to Alan; accordingly, when Mrs Jefferson approached him for credit he had politely but firmly refused. He was horrified a few days later when a gleeful Mrs Jefferson contacted him and informed him that his supervisor – the very person who had given him the original instruction – had in fact granted her the credit she'd requested.

Alan went immediately to his supervisor and – remembering the need to explain how he felt – said: 'I have been placed in an extremely difficult position. Having carried out your orders and refused Mrs Jefferson credit, I find that you have granted it. This makes me appear and feel foolish. Perhaps there has been a change in her credit rating which I do not know about? I would be most grateful if you would tell me how I am to act in such situations in the future.'

It was then up to the supervisor to explain the situation and state how she wanted to proceed in the future – an explanation which Alan could confirm by paraphrasing it back to her to ensure that they both understood the situation.

# Sexual Harassment

More and more reports of sexual harassment in the workplace have come to light in recent years as an increasing number of cases brought before tribunals make people realize that they need not put up with such treatment. Nor is it only women who suffer this unwanted attention.

119

Some of the signs of sexual harassment include:

- personal remarks about sex in general or about an individual's looks or body, etc.
- telling lewd jokes or showing pornographic material;
- propositions, whether direct or indirect;
- suggestive comments or gestures;
- any unwanted and unnecessary physical contact.

There are some instances where jobs or promotion are offered in return for sexual favours. If the relevant person in authority knows about this and does nothing about it, he can be said to have condoned the practice.

Should you feel that you are a victim of sexual harassment, there are various steps you can take:

- You must make clear from the outset that you do not like or want such behaviour. (By doing so, you will ensure that even the 'friendly toucher' realizes that you do not enjoy such familiarity and will stop).
- Make what is happening obvious to others, even if you feel that your position makes this difficult. Those who deliberately indulge in sexual harassment don't usually want everyone else to know about it. One young woman I know was sitting with colleagues around a boardroom table when she felt a hand squeezing her knee. Turning to the man beside her, she took hold of his sleeve, lifting his arm, and said loudly enough for others to hear, 'I believe this is yours; please keep it to yourself.'
- It is an unfortunate fact that some people (men and women) take pleasure in embarrassing those who are younger or more vulnerable than themselves. They may do this by telling smutty jokes or giving graphic descriptions of their latest (real or imagined) sexual escapades. If you don't enjoy this, you don't have to listen. It is best if you can say something like 'I really don't wish to hear this.' If you find this really difficult, just quietly (but patently) walk away.
- Let those around you know what is going on. At work you can

tell colleagues; if the situation arises at home, speak to a friend or relative who can be supportive. With someone else by your side you will find it easier to confront your aggressor.

- Another good reason for talking to other people is to see whether they too are on the receiving end of sexual harassment. A complaint made by several people is likely to carry more weight and bring about a more immediate response than one by a single individual.

- If the problem continues, keep a written record of instances of harassment – including such details as dates and times, whether or not anyone else was present, etc.

- If no action is taken, write a letter stating the facts as you see them and your objection to the behaviour. Send one copy to the offender, one to his supervisor and keep one for your records.

- Keep a note of what action is or is not taken. If there is to be an investigation, ask to be kept informed of its progress.

- In extreme cases you may decide to contact your union, an industrial tribunal or even the police. This is particularly important if the harassment continues away from the workplace as well as within it.

# CHAPTER NINE

# Being in Authority

Having looked at occasions when you have to deal with others in authority, there will of course be times when *you* will find yourself in a supervisory position. It may be as a department head or manager in a work situation; it may be as a team or group leader; or perhaps you are a parent with responsibility for one or more children. For the purposes of this chapter, whichever your role I am going to refer to you as a 'supervisor'.

The first essential for any supervisor in any field is to be a good communicator. You must be able to give and receive information, to state clearly just what you want and why you want it. You also need to listen actively to any feedback you may receive – pleasant or not. The more you are able to discuss matters with those whom you lead, the better the atmosphere will be and the more likely you are to achieve your aims. An increase in supervisory input, where those whom you lead are told not only *what* you want them to do but *why*, will lead to extra loyalty and effort on everyone's part.

Whatever your personal status, it is vital to maintain good relations with all other levels – those whom you supervise, your colleagues and (if in business) your own management.

If you desire loyalty from those around you, you must be loyal to them in return. Credit should be given to those who deserve it and any praise passed on to the relevant people. Too many leaders are willing to accept praise from outside on behalf of the group as a whole without ever passing it on to the rest of the team.

Not only is this unfair but it is likely to deter individuals from making extra effort in the future – after all, what is the point if no one is going to notice?

As a supervisor you will naturally be approached by others who seek your help with their problems. (In some cases, having realized that a problem exists you may have to be the one to make the first move.) To retain the loyalty and trust of these people, you should try and help them deal with these problems without yourself running to pass it on to someone else, unless you feel this is absolutely essential. Even in such cases, the person with whom you are dealing should be told that this is what you believe to be in his best interests and you should seek his permission if at all possible. There will also be times when you might feel that outside help would be beneficial and so, although you cannot compel anyone to seek it, you can do your best to persuade him to do so.

Leading others involves many skills. You should be able to:

- delegate fairly
- motivate other people
- ensure their commitment by demonstrating your own
- be seen to be facing difficulties rather than running away from them
- represent your team to higher authority if necessary
- be seen to be pulling your own weight

Delegating, of course, does not mean opting out of the work yourself. Your position may mean that you are responsible for the standard attained by the whole team but, as an individual you are also responsible for yourself and what you achieve personally.

In any group situation, whether work- or family-based, there are bound to be disagreements and differences of opinion. In such cases it is up to you as the leader to avoid becoming personally involved and to act as mediator, doing your best to ensure that things are running smoothly again as soon as possible. This involves not only being fair but being *seen* to be fair – even when your own natural inclination or previous experience leads you to believe one person more than another. Each party concerned must be given the opportunity to put his own side of the story – although it is better if this is not done in front of everyone else, particularly if some sort of disciplinary action may become necessary. Should you find such problems arising with increasing frequency, it may be time to try to look below the surface to see if you can discover some underlying cause.

If you are in a position of authority, you will accept that there are bound to be times when others approach you wanting to discuss their problems. This is something for which any good leader should be prepared. In fact, if it never happens it means that the members of your team either are not seeing you as their leader or that they have no confidence in you. Naturally you will not be able to find a solution to every problem, but you should be able to help them find a person (or organization) who can.

Because a supervisor is also seen as an advisor, you must be able to take a genuine interest in every member of the group – even those with whom you do not feel a natural empathy. There is no way in which you can solve someone else's problem but you can offer advice and understanding and help him to find a means of solving it for himself. It would be stating the obvious to say that any counselling or assistance with personal (as opposed to work-related) problems should be carried out in complete confidence. You may advise him to speak to someone else but you cannot do it for him.

The role of counsellor or advisor is never an easy one, but there are a few basic rules that should always be borne in mind:

- Strict confidence should always be observed.
- Listen well to whatever you are told and respond with the type of feedback that makes it clear that you have understood.
- Give whatever advice you feel able to give – even if it is not what the person really wants to hear – trying always to make it as positive as possible.
- If you feel that you are unable or unqualified to help further, tell him this and offer to introduce him to someone else who may be able to help him.

# Delegation

Delegating involves finding the person who is best able to do a particular aspect of your job, briefing him on what is required – and then letting him get on with it! Many people find it difficult to let go of a particular task; perhaps they like to believe that no one else could possibly do it as well as they can. Remember the old saying that 'the graveyard is full of indispensable men' and that, although no one really likes to think that his world would go on turning without him, it would do so. A family may grieve for the loss of a parent – but the children will still grow up. A multi-national company's position on the stock-market may be temporarily affected if the chairperson suddenly drops dead at his or her desk – but in all probability the long-term future of that company will not be noticeably damaged.

If you feel that you could not possibly delegate any of the tasks before you, ask yourself whether you have surrounded yourself with the right people. Sometimes, of course, this is beyond your control but, particularly in a business situation, if you have reached a position of authority it should be possible for you to have some voice when it comes to the promotion or selection of the staff with whom you are to work and whom you will be in a position to supervise.

No one could claim that there is not some element of risk involved when handing over a task to another person – but it is a risk you must be prepared to take. It can be minimized by careful advance planning, by the selection of the most appropriate person and by sufficient explanation and training. You will have to realize that the individual to whom the task is new is unlikely to be as quick or efficient at completing it as you would – so allow him a little extra time.

If the task is a complicated one, you may find it easier to explain the concept as a whole at the outset and then to give any precise instructions in smaller chunks so that you are able to check on his accuracy and ability as he goes along. This will also give him a chance to offer you feedback in the form of queries or requests for further explanation, and this in turn will reduce the likelihood of error.

Asking someone to do something which is new to him is likely to involve training; the organization or provision of this training is your responsibility. As the leader of the team, the buck stops with you and you will be held responsible if things go wrong. Remember that certain tasks may seem simple to you (especially if you have been carrying them out for a long time) but they will be new – and therefore difficult – to somebody else.

Once you are happy in your own mind that the other person is sufficiently able to do the job (even if, in your heart, you never quite believe that he does it as well as you used to), you will be free to concentrate your own efforts on those tasks that other people are not in a position to perform. That is what leadership is all about.

## Training

In the area of training, preparation is vital – whether you are dealing with difficult people or not. You need to decide which people to select and what it is that you want them to learn.

Allow ample time – more than you think necessary – for any training programme. You need to have time for explanation, demonstration, feedback in the form of queries and questions and checking or testing. Remember that there is no virtue in making someone endure training sessions of great length with no breaks. It has been shown that we retain best what we learn at the beginning and the end of a studying period. If you break the session up into several short periods (preferably of no more than 30 to 40 minutes each) you will be providing many such 'beginnings' and 'ends'.

If the task to be learned is more than just a basic one, divide it into manageable pieces, taking the time first to explain the relevance of each piece, just *why* the trainee needs to know it and how it fits into the whole scheme of things. Allow the trainee to assimilate and demonstrate his understanding of one section at a time. Give him an opportunity to be a participant rather than simply a listener. Encourage him to use as many of his senses as possible during the training session as this will enable him to retain more. It has been shown that, after a lapse of three days, we remember 10 per cent of what we hear, 20 per cent of what we see and 65 per cent of what we see *and* hear.

Not only should you be sure to allow sufficient time for the training process itself, it is better not to spring someone's training on him suddenly. Give him adequate notice that he is to be taught something new as this allows him time to give feedback of his own. Don't put him under excessive pressure by saying 'I want you to do x, y, z in 10 minutes.' After all, *you* need to know that he understands what is involved.

Do what you can to avoid external distractions such as excessive noise, too high or low a room temperature, a constantly ringing telephone or too many other things going on at the same time. It is because of such distractions that many organizations prefer to conduct training away from their own premises if this is appropriate.

You will also need to accept that we are all made differently and that some people – however intelligent they may be – are slower learners than others. All the impatience in the world will not change this; indeed, if you are dealing with someone who is nervous or lacking in confidence, a display of impatience on your part will simply make him worse.

Of course the trainee is likely to make mistakes – you probably did too, at first. Provided they are not too enormous, mistakes can prove to be a valid part of the learning process; your trainee will become aware of what *not* to do and this will assist him in remembering what he *must* do. At the same time he can be shown how to correct any errors he might make in future.

To avoid problems when training others, use the following as a guide:

- Take time to decide who should be trained and in what skill.
- Prepare well, incorporating visual aids and participation where possible. Make it enjoyable for all parties.
- Explain the relevance of what is to be taught and its part in the concept as a whole.

- Break the subject down into manageable chunks.
- If you wish to generate enthusiasm among trainees, you must be enthusiastic yourself.
- Vary the pace and method of training to keep the trainee(s) interested.
- Allow plenty of time for feedback and questions.
- Don't begin part two until you are sure the trainee(s) understands part one.
- Use errors positively.

## Motivation

If you are in a position of authority part of your job is to motivate those around you. Without effective motivation things will not just stay the same – they will actually deteriorate. Positivity attracts positivity and negativity attracts negativity, so how you feel and the enthusiasm you are able to generate are of vital importance if you wish to see enthusiastic behaviour on the part of other members of the team.

Remember that anyone who makes the effort to do something well – from the child laying the table for the first time to the engineer who designs a new component – deserves to have that effort recognized. If you do not actually thank him or find some other way of making him aware that he is appreciated for what he has achieved, he is unlikely to be willing to try so hard in the future. You may even succeed in making him into a difficult person. Never assume that other people will realize automatically how much their efforts are appreciated – very few of us are mind-readers and in any case we all like to be told.

Just as there are occasions when it is appropriate for you to delegate tasks, others should be offered that opportunity, too. This is not the same thing as allowing them to avoid their duties. However, learning to delegate is an integral part of development and should be encouraged where possible.

Use training techniques to explain to other people how you

would like them to do things. By observing their abilities you will begin to have more confidence in them. They, in turn, will be aware of this and their own self-confidence will grow. We all get far more pleasure from what we do when we know we do it well.

While some form of supervision may be essential – particularly in the early stages – try and do this from 'one step back' so that no one feels you are hovering over him or watching his every move. Nothing is more likely to induce nervousness and inefficiency – even in those who know what to do. Try and find that happy balance between being available when help is needed and forcing attention on those who do not really want it.

When problems do arise – as of course they are bound to – do what you can to help find solutions as soon as possible. Arguments or conflict situations can destroy motivation and, if one individual becomes demotivated, the feeling can spread quickly to the entire group.

# Leadership

There is no one correct style of leadership. Yours will depend upon the tasks before you and those with whom you have to deal. Leadership is not the same for the president of the local women's institute as for someone who has charge of a group of young offenders. You must choose according to the situation from one of three basic types, each of which has its positive and negative aspects. These types (and their plus and minus factors) are:

## The Commander

This leader gives orders and expects them to be obeyed instantly. He rarely allows an opportunity for feedback or for questions – and if he does he is unlikely to pay any real attention to what is said.

- Plus factors:
  His methods gain an instant response.
  They may be effective in the short term.
  He may give a sense of security to those who come from negative backgrounds.
- Minus factors
  No communication is encouraged.
  Those he leads may become frustrated at being refused an opportunity to contribute.
  He himself may soon feel isolated.

## The Instigator

This is someone who is good at setting things in motion. He tends to inform others of the basic objective and then leave them to work out tasks and methods for themselves. He prefers as little personal involvement in a project as possible.

- Plus factors
  This method allows individuals to develop their own potential.
  Because they make their own choices, team-members' level of commitment is likely to be high.
- Minus factors
  Each project is likely to take a great deal of time.
  Lack of clear direction is likely to lead to feelings of insecurity within the team.

## The Negotiator

This leader involves other people at all stages of a project. He actively encourages feedback in the form of questions or suggestions. He likes other people to contribute their own ideas, which he will judge on their merits and implement if he feels it appropriate – giving credit to the instigator. Despite all this, he still maintains overall responsibility for the task in hand.

- Plus factors
  Because they are involved at all stages, members of the team are likely to be far more motivated and enthusiastic.
  Good communication is encouraged.
  Team members learn to use their own initiative.
- Minus factors
  Additional input may increase the amount of time needed to complete a project.
  Too much discussion could cause the participants to lose sight of the main objectives.
  Because they are able to ask questions and make suggestions, too many possible answers may be provided which could cause confusion.

Although the Commander, the Instigator and the Negotiator each has positive and negative qualities, the one most likely to create a successful team around him, and therefore the one you should try to be, is the Negotiator.

# Difficulties a Leader May Face

However good a leader may be in theory, he is still going to be affected by those difficult people with whom he comes into contact.

## Those with Potential Behaviour or Attitude Problems

These problem people might act aggressively but, because aggressive people often have a great deal of energy and may well be ambitious, it is often worth persevering with them. A good place to start is to try and work out *why* they feel they need to act in the way they do.

**Why?**

- A poor self-image. Perhaps they feel that they have an inferior background or standard of education.
- They believe that they are not being sufficiently 'stretched' by the tasks or duties allotted to them.
- They feel like outsiders (possibly due to race, culture, personality traits, accent, etc.) This does not necessarily imply that they are being treated like outsiders, although this is a possibility you will have to look into.

**What to Do**

- Have a meeting with them and tell them what you would like them to do, explaining how their roles fit in with the wider concept of the project and the importance of their own particular input.
- Let them know the standards you wish them to achieve, assuring them of your confidence in their ability to reach those standards – both because of their training and experience of because of the type of people they are.
- Actively encourage feedback and listen to what they say, indicating that you would be willing to incorporate any valid suggestions.
- Do what you can to encourage team feeling and co-operation so that they feel themselves part of the project as a whole.
- Show genuine appreciation of the work they do. A potentially aggressive person treated in this way is likely to throw himself wholeheartedly into future tasks.
- Encourage them to progress even higher up the ladder and offer to help them do so.

## Those Who Do Not Like Change

There are some people who are naturally reluctant to make changes, whether these changes affect their own role or the general methods used. Such people can, of course, hold up the progress of an entire project.

## Why?

- Their background may have caused them to become naturally fearful of anything and everything.
- They may have genuine objections to a particular area of change which they believe to be valid (whether they eventually prove to be or not).
- They may be slow thinkers who take time to come round to any ideas which they find new or different.

## What to Do

- Prepare the ground well in advance. Write down a list of proposed changes, stating the advantages and disadvantages, and give it to them at the first possible opportunity.
- Try to think of all the objections they might possibly raise and answer them before they are asked.
- Bring all such members of your team together and go through your written list, pointing out both the positive and negative aspects of each changes. In this way you will gain their trust as they will realize that you are not trying to 'put one over' on them.
- Ask for feedback and listen actively to whatever they have to say.
- Don't make them feel small if they tell you of their fears and doubts – take them seriously and do what you can to set their minds at rest and reassure them.
- Should they raise objections, make sure that these are specific and detailed rather than general indications of disapproval. This will help them to think about what they are saying and their attitude in general.
- Try to find a way of overcoming each objection if possible. If you cannot, describe to them any positive benefits and try in this way to win their support.
- Remember that, even after changes have been made this type of person will take time to accept them fully, so it may be necessary for you to keep an eye on the situation for a while.

## Those Who Hold Things Up

Some people 'sit on things' for such a time, taking so long to play their part in the process, that they prevent all others from getting on with their tasks.

**Why?**

- A fear of making mistakes (which could be due to their background).
- Lack of faith (justified or not) in the quality of the training they have received.
- Being the type of people who feel incapable of making decisions.

**What to Do**

- Assuming they are not being deliberately obstructive, you may need to confirm that they understand what is required of them.
- Offer more training if you feel this is necessary.
- Try and observe them in action so that you can get a better idea of where their difficulties lie.
- Encourage them to feel that they are part of the team and just as good as everyone else. Remind them that all team members rely upon one another.
- Be sure to compliment them as they improve.

## Time-wasters

On the one hand, there are deliberate time-wasters who don't really want to get on with their work. On the other, there are those people who are easily sidetracked and find themselves dealing with matters other than the ones they are supposed to be dealing with.

**Why?**

- Perhaps no one ever really explained the rules to them so that they are not quite sure what they are supposed to be doing. Or it could be that the one doing the explaining *assumed* they had grasped what was said without asking for feedback, whereas there had, in fact, been an area of misunderstanding.

- They have no understanding of the fact that – in business – time is money. Because they receive the same salary at the end of the week or month, they forget to take into account the actual cost of any particular project.
- They claim that 'everyone does it' so they allow their 10-minute coffee break to last for 20 minutes without realizing that this extra 10 minutes twice a day adds up to nearly two hours lost each week.

## What to Do

- Make sure they understand that wasted time costs money. If this is not a business situation you could explain that wasted time prevents both them and other people from getting on with other things.
- Point out to them that by preventing others from doing their work they are being unfair and disruptive.
- Use the 'carrot and stick' approach by making clear the consequences of their time-wasting – whether this means that they will have less opportunity to do those things they really want to do or that they might miss out when it comes to selection for promotion, bonuses, etc.

## Those Who Are Absent More than Seems Appropriate

In every area – schools, businesses, committees, etc. – there are people who seem to take every opportunity to be absent. While one person will take to his bed as soon as he sneezes, another will crawl to work with a temperature of 104°F – probably because he believes that nothing will function effectively unless he is there to keep an eye on things. Although the second type is not to be encouraged as, if he manages to infect everyone else, no work will be done at all, it is the former we are concerned with here.

## Why?

- Some people are so greatly affected by the stresses and pressures around them that they become negative and soon feel genuinely under par, even though there may be nothing physically wrong with them.
- There are those who have statutory paid sick leave and some (although fortunately only a minority) look on this as an extra holiday and make sure that they take it.
- Excessively nervous people may be so fearful of performing badly that they stay away hoping that a troublesome situation will have resolved itself by the time they return.

## What to Do

- The first thing is to try and discover the cause of the absenteeism if possible – particularly if you suspect that it is not due to genuine illness. See if you can establish any regular factor – is it always the same day of the week, or always when they are faced with the same task or are in contact with the same person, etc.?
- If the absenteeism occurs frequently, try telephoning their home during the day. You can explain by saying you wanted to see how they were feeling and whether they've an idea of when they will be able to return. If no one is ever there to answer the telephone, you may have reason to be suspicious.
- Encourage a team spirit so that everyone feels that he has an important role to play in the project, then such people will be less likely to let others down unnecessarily.
- Many companies are now introducing staff counselling as a way of combating absenteeism. This advisory service is usually carried out by outside counsellors rather than by personnel or welfare officers within the company. The reason for this is that – particularly in times of frequent job losses – workers might be reluctant to confide in an 'inside' counsellor since they won't want to appear to be a weak link (and therefore possibly first in line when redundancies are being considered). In addition, it is often easier to talk to a complete outsider than

to someone who knows your colleagues and friends. Participating companies have found that absenteeism has been dramatically reduced (and the efficiency and motivation of those working has usually noticeably increased).

- Keep a note of those who are absent frequently. If you find that A has been away 'due to illness' on eight separate occasions this year, then there is a problem. This is not being underhanded, as you can then help the person concerned by taking him aside and, if the problem turns out to be genuine, point him in the right direction to get help. On the other hand, if he is malingering, he will thus be made aware that you've noticed and are keeping count!

## Those with Prejudices Against You

There are still people who find any reason they can to be resentful of those in authority. Before you take the situation too personally, consider whether this is their general attitude to everyone who holds a senior position.

### Why?

- Perhaps such people have grown up with negative prejudices; these could relate to sex, race, age, etc. Racial prejudice can show itself in two ways: someone from an ethnic minority group might feel that he has been unjustly passed over for promotion, while someone who holds bigoted views may resent having a person from a minority group in authority over him. Similarly, it is not only some men who dislike the thought that a woman is their supervisor; some women cling to the old-fashioned concept that men should at all times be the ones in charge.
- An older man or woman might resent being told what to do by someone who is several years his or her junior.
- If you have been promoted from within the team, another member might feel that he would have been a more suitable choice.

**What to Do**

- Confront the individual in private and ask him to explain his attitude and, if it is personal to you, to tell you why. This could be a helpful exercise in that, especially if you are new to the position, you might be coming across differently than you want to. If he is unable to come up with a valid reason, you will have put him on the spot and he will not be able to carry on in the same way in future without being very conscious of his attitude and behaviour.

- If there is a prejudice, see if you can discover what it is. For example, in one company I researched a certain man did not like the fact that a younger woman had been put in charge of the team. He felt that if she praised him he was being patronized, yet he resented her if she failed to acknowledge his ability. It was only when she discussed the matter with him that he realized he was putting her in an impossible situation where she could do nothing right.

## Those Who Repeatedly Make Errors

All of us make mistakes from time to time, but what you are looking for here is a pattern of mistake after mistake.

**Why?**

- Perhaps these people were not adequately trained in the first place or the trainer failed to give them an opportunity to offer feedback so that they started off from a position of misunderstanding.

- Are their jobs so unstimulating that they have become bored with them?

- They may simply have too much work to do and, in trying desperately to please, they are rushing it and therefore making repeated mistakes.

- Sometimes there are too many people issuing orders at the same time so that they do not know whose wishes take priority yet they do not like to complain.

- If their concentration is poor and there is a disruptive person around (whether in the workplace, the home or the classroom), they may become easily distracted.

**What to Do**

- Realize, first of all, that very few people deliberately go out of their way to produce poor-quality work – and it is usually easy to spot those who do because of their attitude in general.
- Use your powers of observation and monitor the situation.
- Speak to the individual concerned and ask whether he has any particular problems – even if they do not relate to the task itself. Remember the positive-negative-positive formula: begin by saying something pleasant or complimentary ('I realize how much effort you've been putting in'), then identify the problem ('but you do seem to have been making rather a lot of mistakes lately'); finally, bearing in mind that it is never a good thing to leave someone feeling negative, end with a positive comment ('once you've sorted out the problem, I know you'll be producing excellent results again').
- Offer further training or instruction if he feels he needs it.
- If there is a disruptive person around, suggest either that you will have a word with him or (if appropriate) that you will reorganize things so that the two do not come into frequent contact during working hours.
- If you feel that he is being overloaded with work, let him know that you understand the position and will do what you can to find someone to help him, whether on a temporary or a permanent basis.
- If the errors are the result of excessive carelessness, explain the value of his particular role and the part he plays in the project as a whole. Appeal to his own sense of pride in his achievements.

## People Who Are Excessively Untidy

While it is not essential for everything to be neat and precise if good work is to be the result, excessive untidiness can create chaos in a comparatively short time.

## Why?

- Such people simply may not realize that neatness is important. There is always the person who will claim 'I know just where everything is' – until you ask him to find something!
- Things have got so bad that they just cannot face the mammoth clearing-up session necessary to put them right again.
- Their morale is low and they are feeling negative – perhaps because they do not like the work or feel that they are no good at it.

## What to Do

- Explain that, although we all need our things around us during the day, a really messy area indicates a fairly untidy mind and it is actually far harder to think clearly when faced with absolute chaos.
- Encourage them to keep things in order by suggesting that they finish five minutes earlier each day and use those last minutes to straighten their work area.
- Remind them that, should they become ill, someone else may have to take over their tasks – and the untidier their area the more difficult this will be.
- See if you can discover a reason for the chaos. Are they trying to look busier than they are or do they believe that they can avoid some of the pressures of work if they have to spend time hunting for each item they need?
- Make sure that you set a good example! You can hardly complain about other people's untidiness if your own area is all in a heap.

## Personality Conflicts

Friction between two or more personalities in any team affects not only the people immediately concerned but every other member of the team as well. Morale will be lowered, work will be affected and output reduced.

## Why?

- Two individuals might dislike each other – either with or without good reason.
- Someone could have been on a level with you at one time and suddenly, there you are, supervising him.
- One person might be going through a difficult time in his personal life. This is probably affecting him emotionally and causing him to act unreasonably towards one or more of those around him.

## What to Do

- Call both/all parties together and see if you can persuade them to discuss their differences calmly in front of you. If you are involved, remember that you cannot force anyone else to change and, though it may be difficult, you can *always* change your own behaviour should you wish to do so. Try to avoid getting personal; remaining objective and fair is one of the necessities of positive leadership.
- If you are newly promoted, approach each former peer in turn and, explaining that you will need his co-operation, ask whether you can count on his support. Most people will be happy to give it and you will soon sense who, if anyone, is going to be difficult.
- If someone is having emotional problems, see if you can arrange for him to have outside counselling.

Being the person in charge is never easy. But the problem does not exist that cannot be handled, and handled sensitively. You will face many challenges but you will grow in confidence and ability with each one you meet and overcome.

# CHAPTER TEN

# Step-by-Step Guide to Dealing with Difficult People

## Understanding Yourself and Others

Study your own reactions to other people; do they follow a pattern? Don't allow yourself to be manipulated – particularly by someone who is difficult towards everybody. Feeling anger is natural; it is the way you *express* it that can be harmful or helpful. Are you the one who always ends up being hurt by your own anger?

Consider how you respond to other people's anger (whether justified or not) and criticism. Consider, too, your own attitudes: are you constantly in a negative frame of mind? Try listing the positive and negative aspects of your life. List those things about yourself that you like.

You might also want to think about emotions: do you find it difficult to express your feelings – both good and bad? Or are you the type of person who goes ahead and says what you feel without taking into account the effect your words have on other people?

Check your personality type to see where changes may need to be made. If you have a poor self-image or low self-esteem, think back to important relationships in childhood – with parents, teachers or others close to you. Try to understand the link between these relationships and your present opinion of yourself.

Remember that your self-image is not fixed – you have the ability to change it. Don't spend too much time looking back on failures but remember any and all your successes – however minor.

Practise visualization techniques in order to create your own future successes.

# Styles of Behaviour

There are three principal behaviour styles – aggressive, submissive and assertive. You should be working towards becoming an assertive person.

## The Aggressive Person

- is intent on satisfying his own needs
- enjoys the feeling of power but is inwardly aware that he is taking advantage of others
- repeats constantly that he is in the right but hides an inner sense of insecurity and doubt
- is often isolated as his behaviour drives others away; yet he will never admit that he wants friends
- is usually energetic but often in a destructive way
- does not really like himself so creates negativity around him
- has the ability to demoralize and humiliate others
- can be recognized by typical verbal and non-verbal (body) language

## The Submissive Person

- is easily put upon by others (and encourages this attitude)
- suffers greatly from a sense of insecurity and feelings of inferiority which are reinforced whenever he comes into contact with an aggressive person
- is often very angry with himself because he knows he lets others take advantage of him
- is expert at hiding his true feelings

- is shy and withdrawn in company
- cannot accept compliments
- suffers from excess stress so has little energy or enthusiasm for anything
- has an attitude that eventually causes others to become irritated with him
- drains other people's energy
- can be recognized by typical verbal and body language

## The Assertive Person

- is concerned for his own and other people's rights
- usually ends up achieving his goals
- has respect for others so is willing to negotiate and compromise where appropriate
- always keeps his promises
- is able to express his true feelings in such a way that, even when they are negative he does not create resentment in others
- feels at peace with himself and others
- is prepared to take risks; if they do not work out, he accepts that making mistakes is part of the learning process
- acknowledges his own failures *and* his successes
- is enthusiastic and can motivate others
- feels good about himself, making other people feel good too
- can be recognized by typical verbal and body language

You can begin to be an assertive person by tackling small problems first, rewarding yourself for what you achieve. Creative visualization helps: consider situations in which you have not acted assertively in the past and ask yourself what you would do differently in future.

Remember that an assertive person can do the following:

- express positive feelings
- express negative feelings
- say no

- give an honest opinion
- say that he is angry, when justified
- preserve his rights while allowing others to preserve theirs
- set goals and be prepared to work towards them, even if they have to be modified along the way
- give genuine compliments and be prepared to accept them, too
- select the ways in which he would like to change himself and work towards doing so
- become a good communicator
- develop the ability to negotiate, compromising where necessary and appropriate
- learn to deal with put-downs
- understand that criticism falls into two categories – fair and unfair – and then:

> ignore that which is unfair
> agree with whatever is justified (but not respond to judgemental statements)
> if the criticism is partly exaggerated, respond only to the justified part
> if the criticism is personal, try responding with a question

# Types of Problem People

You cannot change other people, but you can learn how to handle them.

Type 1 is always concerned with himself, ignoring other people's opinions and feelings.

**What to Do**

- make an appointment to speak to him
- make him feel well disposed towards you
- explain what he does, assuring him that you don't think he does it on purpose
- offer to help him break the pattern

145

Type 2 always leaves you feeling negative and miserable and is basically insecure, with a poor self-image.

## What to Do

- don't apologize or agree
- avoid snapping back
- ask an assertive question
- ignore blustering

Type 3 is aggressive and noisy; likely to stamp, bang the table, shout, etc. He is intent on getting his own way but is usually also a logical thinker. He is good at solving problems but tends to make snap decisions and then to insist on sticking to them.

## What to Do

- stand up to him but avoid getting into a fight
- tell him you disagree but ask him to explain his views further
- don't let him interrupt you
- avoid sounding weak or angry
- maintain eye contact and keep your body language assertive

Type 4 is surreptitiously aggressive, preferring to go behind people's backs with criticism rather than dole it out face-to-face. He likes to make jokes at other people's expense and loves an audience.

## What to Do

- get him alone so that he has no audience
- ask him if he intended to be hurtful
- if you hear what he has said from a third party, ask that person to give you full details; then confront him with what you know and ask whether he meant what he said
- suggest that in future he makes his comments directly to you, in private

Type 5 starts by being pleasant but then loses control; any amount of pressure makes him feel threatened. He is insecure so feels that he needs to attack first.

**What to Do**

- keep eye contact and remain silent until he runs out of steam
- tell him you want to know what he is saying
- find a place to be alone with him and then let him have time to cool down
- ask what is troubling him
- offer help and, if accepted, provide it

Type 6 (A & B) can never make up his mind; 6A thinks he is more efficient than anyone else and does not trust other people's abilities; 6B wants to be helpful but is frightened of doing something wrong.

**What to Do**

- give 6A a deadline, explaining the reason for it
  back everything up with facts and details
- find out why 6B is worried
  discuss his problems with him
  reassure him when you think he is right

Type 7 is very depressing to have around. He always anticipates the worst outcome to any situation and never likes any of the ideas put forward – but he refuses to come up with any alternatives.

**What to Do**

- don't waste time arguing with him
- try not to let him make you feel negative too
- ask him why he feels as he does
- ask him to suggest a solution
- find out what are his worst fears
- tell him you intend to go ahead and will do so alone if necessary

Type 8 thinks everyone or everything is to blame but him. He feels powerless to change things and generally makes life miserable for everyone around him.

**What to Do**

- don't agree with him, apologize or make excuses
- try and get him into a problem-solving frame of mind
- interrupt any of his negative speeches at the first opportunity
- paraphrase what he has said (but only his criticisms, not his judgements, which should be ignored)
- ask problem-solving questions and see if he can offer a positive solution

Type 9 hopes that if he keeps quiet, people will stop asking him questions. He remains silent intentionally, either (i) to exert power or (ii) because he is genuinely confused.

**What to Do**

- start a conversation as soon as possible
- begin with a trivial comment to make him feel at ease
- ask an open question
- remain silent as long as possible, keeping your body language open and friendly
- if you have to break the silence, don't start a fresh conversation, just comment on how ridiculous the situation seems
- then, if necessary, become silent again
- if he starts to talk, don't interrupt
- if he seems anxious, say so and ask why
- tell him what you intend to do and give him a deadline for letting you know what is bothering him

Type 10 believes he knows better than everyone else. Although usually thorough and efficient at work he is a disaster at personal relationships since he is aggressive and a verbal bully.

**What to Do**

- make sure you do your homework before tackling him
- ask for a detailed explanation, listen actively and paraphrase it back to him

- suggest that you'd like to be able to take your problems to him in future
- ask yourself whether working or having a relationship with him is really worth the effort

Type 11 *believes* he knows better than everyone else but does not. He is anxious to gain the respect and friendship of others but is not really prepared to make any effort to do so.

### What to Do

- tackle him on his own
- state your understanding of the facts, allowing him to save face
- if you cannot avoid doing this in front of others, fill the silence with a comment of your own to avoid awkwardness

Type 12 is pleasant and agreeable but completely unreliable; he wants to be liked and needed so he agrees to undertake anything. He truly intends to do what he promises but takes on too much so that he cannot.

### What to Do

- let him know that you like him as a person
- pay him positive compliments (making sure they are genuine)
- tell him you value his opinion and ask for his ideas
- try and discover his real feelings

## Handling Conflict

Conflict is natural and healthy when it involves ideas but can be negative when it becomes a clash of personalities. It can have both positive and negative aspects and outcomes.

- listen actively to what others say
- try and understand the reason for other people's behaviour
- allow others to say what they feel but ask them to do so assertively rather than aggressively

- if a conflict cannot be prevented, it must be resolved as positively as possible

With regard to conflict, most people fall into one of four basic categories:

## The Processor

- has an analytical mind
- is more interested in the task than the people involved
- is accurate and efficient but can be unimaginative and boring
- can be left to make and carry out plans
- is not necessarily a quick thinker
- needs to be presented with facts and logic if you are to win him over

## The Dictator

- whose most important word is 'I'
- can be very aggressive, wanting everything done immediately
- is often impatient and intolerant
- is more interested in outcomes than individuals
- is a high achiever with no self-doubt
- is a controller of others and a verbal bully
- needs to be confronted assertively or he will lose all respect for you

## The Enthuser

- can be aggressive but is quite people-orientated
- is charismatic, with a need to be popular which is usually fulfilled
- has a high level of energy and enthusiasm which he cannot always sustain
- motivates others well
- needs those around him to be enthusiastic

## The Empathizer

- is kind and caring but not too good at getting things done
- can be a procrastinator and indecisive

- is a loyal supporter but not a good leader
- acts submissively under stress: don't put him under pressure; show him you like him instead

Conflict can cause excess stress which may result in negative defensive reactions. Remember that it is not opposing ideas that cause problems, but opposing people.

## Communicating Effectively

Verbal communication is more effective than written communication. It involves transmitting a message and receiving feedback. Eighty per cent of a message is received through body language. Remember to take into account the current attitudes and level of understanding of your listeners.

Active listening involves making sense of what the speaker intends to transmit and proving you have understood by offering feedback.

Feedback involves paraphrasing what has been said to demonstrate your comprehension, asking questions or asking for clarification, explaining how the message makes you feel and offering positive criticism. If you are the speaker, it is up to you to ask for feedback.

Being an active listener means concentrating on what is being said. You must accept that the speaker has the right to his views whether or not you agree with them. Avoid anticipating what he is about to say, offer feedback and pay attention to his body language.

An effective speaker remains assertive. You must constantly adjust your mode of communication to your listener's state of awareness. Be clear, leaving no room for misunderstanding. Use appropriate language and request feedback and listen actively to it. Make sure that your body language reinforces what you are saying.

### Body language

Body language can be positive in that it transmits our present state of mind and emotion, it reinforces what we say and can even replace the verbal message.

151

Body language can also be negative: it can mislead listeners about how we feel and can contradict our verbal message or be so confusing that no message is received. Try to practise assertive body language and if you want to attempt mirroring make sure it doesn't become pure mimicry.

# Saying No

Saying no is never easy, but you must learn how. Ask yourself why you find it difficult and consider the possible outcomes: what is the worst that can happen?

Remember that the only way to say no and retain your self-respect is to be assertive about it. You have a right to say no; you may or may not choose to give an explanation (which is not the same thing as an excuse). Saying no involves:

- asking yourself whether you want to
- asking for further details of the request if you need them
- keeping your refusal short and making no apologies
- offering some other sort of help if you want to do so

## Why You Might Find Saying No Difficult

- lack of self-esteem
- negative self-image
- guilt
- the need to be liked

# Dealing with Complaints

- remain calm at all times, whether the complaint is fair or not
- practise physical relaxation
- let the complainer run out of steam

- listen actively – and make the complainer aware of this
- show empathy by giving positive feedback
- offer to look into the matter
- if there is a mistake, admit it and apologize before saying how you suggest putting it right
- don't make excuses
- if the complainer is being deliberately difficult or aggressive, be sure to remain assertive
- be sure to keep pen and paper beside the telephone
- if you need to interrupt, always call the complainer by name
- if you cannot deal with the complaint on the spot, tell the complainer when you will ring back – and do so
- if you cannot deal with it personally, explain this and say that you will contact the relevant person, who will then ring the complainer back – and check to make sure this is done

# Coping with Authority

- if you always have difficulty with authority figures, look to your past to see if you can discover the reason
- if you feel you are being held back, act assertively; script the situation in advance and choose an appropriate moment to broach the subject
- if you receive only criticism and never praise, explain how this makes you feel
- a vague or confused authority is worse than none at all
- if you are faced with contradictory requests, make sure you confront both superiors, if only to make one aware that the other is trying to undermine him
- an authority figure who does not support his team will lose all trust and respect

### Aggressive Verbal Tactics

- sarcasm
- public criticism

- temper tantrums
- silent treatment
- put-downs

### Sexual Harassment

- making personal remarks
- telling lewd jokes or displaying pornographic material
- direct or indirect propositions
- suggestive comments or gestures
- unwanted physical contact

### Dealing with Harassment

- make your objection known immediately
- see whether anyone else has been bothered
- keep a written record of instances of harassment
- if no action is taken, write a letter, keeping copies
- keep a note of any action taken
- in extreme cases, be prepared to take the matter further

# Being in Authority

## A Good Leader Can

- be a good communicator
- maintain a good relationship with all other levels
- be loyal to those around him, giving praise where it is due
- delegate
- motivate
- demonstrate his own commitment
- be seen to face difficulties
- represent the team
- be seen to be pulling his weight
- take an interest in each member of the team
- take responsibility for training (whether or not he does it himself)

The three basic styles of leadership are:

## The Commander

- gives orders
- does not allow opportunity for feedback

## The Instigator

- good at setting things in motion
- lets others work out methods for themselves
- tries not to become personally involved

## The Negotiator

- involves others at all stages
- encourages feedback
- maintains overall responsibility

Try to become a Negotiator.

## Difficulties a Leader May Face

- people with behaviour or attitude problems
- those who do not like change
- people who delay things
- time-wasters
- persistent absentees
- those who are prejudiced against you
- people who repeatedly make mistakes
- people who are excessively untidy
- conflicting personalities

By facing challenges and difficulties, you, as a leader, will grow in confidence and ability.

# Further Reading and Resources

## Further Reading

Barrat-Godefroy, Stephanie, *How to Develop Charisma and Personal Magnetism* (Thorsons, 1993).

Harris, Thomas, *I'm OK, You're OK* (Pan, 1973).

Lindenfield, Gael, *Assert Yourself* (Thorsons, 1987).

—, *Managing Anger* (Thorsons, 1993).

—, *The Positive Woman* (Thorsons, 1992).

—, *Super Confidence* (Thorsons, 1989).

Markham, Ursula, *Managing Stress* (Element Books, 1989).

McWilliams, Peter, and John-Roger, *Do It!* (Thorsons, 1991).

—, *Life 101* (Thorsons, 1992).

—, *You Can't Afford the Luxury of a Negative Thought* (Thorsons, 1991).

Smith, Manuel J., *When I Say No I Feel Guilty* (Bantam, 1975).

# Self-help

For details of self-help and relaxation cassettes, contact:
The Hypnothink Foundation
PO Box 66
Gloucestershire
GL2 9YG

(Also conducts business training seminars and can offer advice on staff welfare counselling)

# Index

Jane Wilson
1-800 388-7977
MTh 8am 7pm    00122008
FRI 8   5
www. speedtrap.com
SAT

dial pad

✓ ↑ Interest

bankrate.com

— 99 fixed

www.
C7tratv.com

Cyberguy